ORTHO'S All About

Water Gardening

Written by Greg and Sue Speichert

Meredith® Books
Des Moines, Iowa

Ortho® Books
An imprint of Meredith® Books

All About Water Gardening
Writers: Greg and Sue Speichert
Editor: Marilyn Rogers
Technical Consultant: Charles B. Thomas
Contributing Writer: Martin Miller
Art Director: Tom Wegner
Assistant Art Director: Harijs Priekulis
Copy Chief: Catherine Hamrick
Copy and Production Editor: Terri Fredrickson
Book Production Managers: Pam Kvitne,
    Marjorie J. Schenkelberg
Contributing Copy Editors: Jay Lamar, Angela K. Renkoski,
    Barbara Feller-Roth
Contributing Proofreaders: Maria Duryee,
    Kathy Roth Eastman, Beth Lastine
Contributing Illustrator: Mike Eagleton
Contributing Prop/Photo Stylist: Peggy Johnston
Indexer: Donald Glassman
Electronic Production Coordinator: Paula Forest
Editorial and Design Assistants: Kathleen Stevens,
    Karen Schirm

Additional Editorial Contributions from
    Art Rep Services
Director: Chip Nadeau
Designer: lk Design
Illustrator: Rick Hanson

Meredith® Books
Editor in Chief: James D. Blume
Design Director: Matt Strelecki
Managing Editor: Gregory H. Kayko
Executive Ortho Editor: Larry Erickson

Director, Retail Sales and Marketing: Terry Unsworth
Director, Sales, Special Markets: Rita McMullen
Director, Sales, Premiums: Michael A. Peterson
Director, Sales, Retail: Tom Wierzbicki
Director, Sales, Home & Garden Centers: Ray Wolf
Director, Book Marketing: Brad Elmitt
Director, Operations: George A. Susral
Director, Production: Douglas M. Johnston

Vice President, General Manager: Jamie L. Martin

Meredith Publishing Group
President, Publishing Group: Christopher M. Little
Vice President, Finance & Administration: Max Runciman

Meredith Corporation
Chairman and Chief Executive Officer: William T. Kerr
Chairman of the Executive Committee: E.T. Meredith III

Greg and Sue Speichert own Crystal Palace Perennials and publish *Water Gardening Magazine*. Charles B. Thomas is the founder of Lilypons Water Gardens.

Thanks to
Janet Anderson, Kathy Roth Eastman, Karin Holms, Water
    Creations, Inc., Spectrum Communications, Inc.

Photographers
    (Photographers credited may retain copyright ©
    to the listed photographs.)
L = Left, R = Right, C = Center, B = Bottom, T = Top
Debbi Adams: 5C; **William D. Adams:** 39B; **Rudolf
Arndt/Visuals Unlimited:** 64B; **Robert A. Behrstock:** 56T,
59T; **Kate Boykin:** 62T, 72TR; **Rob Cardillo:** 17B, 20R,
22, 23, 24, 25, 26, 27, 28L, 34T, 35BR, 37C, 37B, 38BL,
40TR, 40B, 43T, 43C, 45T, 52, 53, 54, 55, 56C, 56B, 73;
David Cavagnaro: 34B, 36T, 38T, 40TL, 42T, 44C, 44B,
45C, 45B; **Kathy Adams Clark/KAC Productions:** 29T,
29CL, 29CR; **Crandall and Crandall:** 67T; **Marc
Epstein/Visuals Unlimited:** 58; **Catriona Tudor Erler:** 9T,
20L, 61TR; **Derek Fell:** 36C; **Susan M. Glascock:** 32B,
36B, 42B, 63B; **John Glover:** 4, 7TR, 16R, 19TR, 19B, 21T,
35T, 41B, 88; **David Goldberg:** 82, 83; **Anne Gordon:** 32T;
Jerry Harpur: 9B, 11, 15, 28R; **Jessie M. Harris:** 29B, 39T,
57T; **Lynne Harrison:** 35BL, 61BL; **Saxon Holt:** 6T (Chris
Jacobson), 10, 17, 30T, 39C, 70, 75B; **Jerry
Howard/Positive Images:** 14B; **Sally McCrae Kuyper:** 43B;
Andrew Lawson: 5L, 35CB; **Andrew Lawson/Designer:
Wendy Lauderdale:** 14T, 16L; **Hanson Man:** 60TL, 60TR,
60BL; **Maslowski/Visuals Unlimited:** 63C; **Marilynn
McAra:** 7B, 12B, 21BL, 44T; **Bryan McCay:** 74, 84, 85TR,
86, 87; **David McDonald:** 18; **William H. Mullins:** 64T;
Clive Nichols: 59B; **Clive Nichols/Designer: Richard
Coward:** 12TL; **Clive Nichols/Mr. Fraser/J. Treyer-Evans:**
89; **Clive Nichols/Andrew and Karla Newell:** 6B; **Bob
Romar:** 41C; **Jeff Rugg/Pond Supplies of America:** 61C;
John G. Shedd Aquarium: 61TL, 61BR; **John G. Shedd
Aquarium/Patrice Ceisel:** 62B; **John G. Shedd
Aquarium/Edward G. Lines, Jr.:** 60BR; **Richard Shiell:**
33C, 33B, 37T; **Rob and Ann Simpson:** 69; **Garold
Sneegas/Aquatic Kansas Images:** 63T, 65; **Pam
Spaulding/Positive Images:** 7L; **Sue Speichert:** 80, 81;
Albert Squillace/Positive Images: 38BR; **Steve Struse:**
19TL, 31B, 46, 48, 57B, 66, 68, 72B; **Michael S.
Thompson:** 12TR, 32C, 40C, 41T, 42C; **Connie Toops:**
21BR, 33T; **Gary G. Wittstock:** 5R, 76, 77, 78, 79

On the cover: *Nymphaea alba*, a day-blooming hardy water
lily. Joseph Bory Latour-Marliac used this species extensively
in his hybridizing work, making it one of the original
Marliac-type water lilies and the parent of many of today's
hybrids. Photograph by Gary G. Wittstock.

All of us at Ortho® Books are dedicated to providing you
with the information and ideas you need to enhance your
home and garden. We welcome your comments and
suggestions about this book. Write to us at:
    Meredith Corporation
    Ortho Books
    1716 Locust St.
    Des Moines, IA 50309-3023

If you would like more information on other Ortho
products, call 800-225-2883 or visit us at www.ortho.com

THE WONDERFUL WORLD OF WATER GARDENING 4

PLANTS FOR THE WATER GARDEN 18

CRITTERS 58

TAKING CARE OF THE POND 70

PROJECTS 76

A PRIMER FOR WATER GARDEN INSTALLATION 84

4

THE WONDERFUL WORLD OF WATER GARDENING

Water gardening brings a world of wonder and excitement to any backyard. Whether you are a beginning or experienced gardener, you'll find a pond easy to care for and a treasure trove of new sights and sounds for the entire family.

Water gardening is many things. It's gardening, fish-keeping, bird-watching, and nature and habitat restoration. It's part hobby, part educational, part spiritual. Although the pond may be defined by liner and stone, it is ever-changing and waiting to be explored. Each day brings a new surprise or an unseen challenge.

Water gardening can be as easy or complex as you want it to be. People with busy schedules like water gardening because of the ease of care and the satisfying results they get with just monthly feedings and little else. They can enjoy a lush garden and wildlife habitat that almost maintains itself. People new to gardening have learned how easy it is to be a successful water gardener. The bane of most new gardeners is watering: figuring out when to water, how to water, and how much to water. Water gardening eliminates those dilemmas—you can't over-water water plants!

A water garden provides a cool oasis in our hectic lives, a place to retreat to and unwind from the outside world. Water cascading down a waterfall, babbling in a brook, or lying still in a reflective pool soothes the spirit and refreshes the soul. It takes us back to a simpler, less demanding time in our lives. It reminds us of the cabin by the lake and the pond of our youth where we caught frogs and explored for underwater treasures. Water gardening is all that and more.

WATER GARDENS IN HISTORY

Water gardening and water gardens have been around for a long time. This fascination with water can be traced throughout history. The Egyptians planted water lilies for their fragrance and for use in religious ceremonies. Thousands of water lilies were cultivated for

Whether it's lush, exotic plants or schools of beautiful fish, the flutter of birds or the "ribbit" of frogs, everyone will find something that attracts them to water gardening.

the priests, who drank wine through the stems of the native water lilies, for a slightly narcotic experience. Papyrus, a water plant that grows at the margins of ponds or in bogs, was planted and harvested to make scrolls, the precursor to paper.

In Asia, water gardening is even more central to the culture, because many of the area's staple foods are aquatic or semiaquatic. The main food, rice, has been cultivated for thousands of years. Taro (often called elephant's ear) and lotus are just as old and have a special place in water gardens, which represent the heavens to Asians of all classes. In early water gardens, goldfish and koi were objects of wealth and status, possessed mainly by the ruling classes.

The Moors and Turk nobles used water features to cool their surroundings. Muslims developed pools into geometric shapes, and the features became stylized versions of irrigation canals and reservoirs. Later, French and German rulers used water to rival the glory days of the Roman Empire, displaying wealth and power with huge fountains as well as man-made streams, waterfalls, and lakes.

In Victorian times, rulers and the wealthy used water gardens to display the new, exotic plants and animals brought back to England from the four corners of the world. In the United States, 19th-century landscape architects such as Jens Jensen and Frederick Law Olmsted used water in the landscape to bring nature and recreation to the inhabitants of the country's burgeoning cities.

Most homeowners of the time, however, were not able to afford such a luxury as a water garden. Building one took a great deal of time, effort, and money, far more than the average person was willing to invest. Because the pond was usually made from concrete, it was difficult to build irregularly shaped ponds; and once a pond was built, little could be done to change its design or configuration. Moving the pond was out of the question. All this changed in the late 1960s with the advent of flexible liners, which have altered the very nature of water gardening, essentially bringing it to the masses. No longer just for the wealthy rulers of countries, water gardening is for everyone.

THIS BOOK AS YOUR GUIDE

This book leads you through the wonderful world of water gardening. In this first section, you'll discover design ideas for a variety of installations and tips on choosing the right one for you, including where to put a garden on your site, what kind of layout to use, and which plants to grow. It's the individual differences between plants that determine where you place them in the pond and how you plant and propagate them. To help you plan what's best for your site and climate, study the encyclopedia section (pages 22–45), which has detailed information about the kinds of plants and their characteristics. Beginning on page 46, learn how to grow water plants, select a planting medium, and fertilize. Later in the book (pages 58–69), turn your attention to other inhabitants of your pond—both aquatic and two- and four-legged critters. You'll find the fundamentals of pond care and maintenance starting on page 70. For details on prized ponds and a primer on constructing your own, turn to page 76.

With this inspiration and guidance in hand, you soon will have your own heavenly water garden to enjoy.

OPTIONS FOR DESIGN

There's a style of water feature for every landscape. Some gardeners want a natural pond. Others prefer a formal design. Before you decide, plan how you will use the pond. Ponds are classified into three categories: water gardens (including bog gardens), fishponds, and fountains.

WATER GARDENS

Water gardens are the most popular water feature and are what most people think of

Like a tiny oasis, a pond or water garden can be as elegant as this small pool in a secluded patio (above), or as simple as this container holding a watery world of surprises at right.

when they think of a pond. They are designed first and foremost to provide a friendly habitat for aquatic plants. Even with fish and other wildlife in and near the water, the pond is still considered a water garden. If you want to attract birds or other animals to your yard, this is the pond for you.

Popular in Europe and England, water gardens have benefited most from the revolution in liners. Development of flexible liner made it easy to create a pond with the relatively shallow depths required for plants. With flexible liner, water gardens can be built in sun or moderate shade, and they are easier to set up and maintain than fishponds and fountains. If you add a few fish to your water garden, you'll need little, if any, filtration, and you'll have few algae problems.

Water gardens can fit any budget and any size yard. A small plastic washtub set on a porch or balcony and filled with small, floating plants can beautify the tiniest space. For larger landscapes and pocketbooks, you can have almost anything in your water garden, even a recirculating trout stream with live trout. If you're worried about children falling in, build the pond with no open water: Make it shallow, filled with small stones and run by a small pump and fountain, perhaps with a waterfall, or fit a rigid plastic grate just below the water surface.

Water gardens are a must for the birder, because the water and plants attract and benefit a great number of birds. You can create distinct pools—birdbaths—with rocks at different depths to attract different species. This isn't advisable in a fishpond or a fountain, because diseases from the birds infect the fish, and bird feathers can clog a fountainhead. Add streams to attract small birds and small animals such as salamanders and newts.

Low spots in your yard may be perfect for a freestanding bog garden, which is an area for plants that thrive in soil that you—or nature, in this case—keep constantly moist. (These are not the true acidic bogs that are home to cranberries and some carnivorous plants.)

PRIMARILY FISH

A fishpond, by definition, is designed to carry a heavier concentration of fish than a water garden. Fishponds require certain design elements. They must always have adequate filtration and a sufficiently large pump. Also, the bottom of the pond is generally sloped toward center drains that remove settling waste. They must also be designed so that you can easily get in to collect and remove floating debris, which reduces infection and increases water quality.

Fishponds also have special maintenance needs. Although fish and plants are not incompatible, the addition of plants to a fishpond complicates its maintenance. Your fish will need periodic chemical treatments to

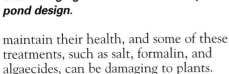

Fishponds move the hobby of raising fish outdoors, often bringing with it the need for special filtration and pond design.

Ponds are a haven for wildlife and a birder's delight. The pebble beach at the end of this pond lets wildlife get close to the water.

maintain their health, and some of these treatments, such as salt, formalin, and algaecides, can be damaging to plants.

If you have plants in your pond, you'll need to use treatments that are plant-safe. Or you can remove the plants before treating the water, or remove the fish and treat them in a clean garbage can or wading pool deep enough to keep them from jumping out. Heavy fish loads in a pond may also require pumping and water movement that might be too strong for some plants. Select sturdy varieties that will withstand the water movement required for the fish.

Keep in mind that koi and goldfish eat plants as well as insects. Large koi can decimate a planted pond in a day, and the more koi you have, the more they eat. They usually start with the most expensive plant you own. Solutions include careful selection of plants for sturdy varieties and careful management of fish populations (see page 60). Besides eating plants, fish also like to root around in the soil of the pots. You can reduce the resulting mess by placing large stones on top of the soil.

If you want both a fishpond and a water garden without these inconveniences, you can install two ponds connected by a stream. Design one pond for plants and the other as a home to goldfish and koi. This resolves many of the filtration and water-quality issues inherent to a fishpond. The pond with plants functions as a mini wetland, absorbing waste from the fish and cleaning the water. That makes the pond healthier and more attractive. The two ponds can be isolated from each other by a waterfall or gate valve, so that when you have to treat the fishpond for disease, you can do it without harming the plants. You can also treat the plants for any pest outbreak without worrying about harming the fish.

FOUNTAINS

Fountain ponds are the simplest water feature, containing only the fountain and water, with no plant or animal life. Installed above ground or in the ground, they often feature a large, central fountain that can shoot water high into the air. Fountainheads are designed to produce a variety of spray patterns—from a simple, single jet to twisting jets darting in and out of the water.

A fountain pond with decorative rock arranged on a metal grate covering the pump is an ideal feature for a family with young children. The fountain of water rises above the rocks, splashes down on them, then falls back into the pond. Because the pond is filled with rock and has no deep water, there is no risk to young children.

In a pond without plants, you can keep the water crystal clear with an algaecide or even simple bleach, which are too strong for plants and animals.

If you want to have plants and a fountain, take care when choosing plants. Also be aware that their placement is critical to their survival. Water lilies, for example, will wither and die if they're placed where the fountain keeps the pads in constant motion.

Fountains, with their soothing sounds, change the mood of a garden, transforming it from a simple group of plants to a focal point.

SELECTING A SITE

Water gardens are now within the budget and skill level of most homeowners who want them, and the tools and materials available today make water garden installation easier than ever. You can put a water garden almost anywhere: in a large, expansive landscape; in a small, urban backyard; or on a balcony or porch. Even so, for the water garden to be successful—and to get the most enjoyment from it—you must put it in the *right* site.

Before you decide on the final location, there are a number of things to keep in mind: your site conditions, including slope, soil, sun, shade, and wind; how you want to use the pond; climatic conditions in your region; and even location of utility lines. Finding the perfect spot requires balancing all of these elements. Here's what to look for.

Ponds should complement and enhance the landscape, fitting into the surrounding scheme and placed where they look most natural. They should also complement your ideas for using the space.

FINDING A SPOT FOR IT

SLOPE: Check out your site. Consider the slope and grade of your yard and work with it. The lowest spot may look like the best place for a pond, but it's actually the worst. Rainwater flows into a low-lying pond, muddying the water, rinsing out your fish and knocking over plants. Poor drainage can also cause runoff to well up underneath the pond liner, creating bubbles which rise to the surface and look as though the Loch Ness monster found its way into your pond. Placing the pond just above the lowest spot avoids these problems.

If your site slopes, you'll have to put in some extra time preparing it for the water garden. You'll need to level it, either by grading it and building a retaining wall or by building up the downhill side of the pond by adding soil or rock. Otherwise, water will run out of the pond and down the hill.

Fortunately, a sloped site has its benefits, too. It's a perfect spot to add a waterfall, and you can lay out a slope to include a stream that runs from an upper pond to a lower one. When building on a slope, make sure you have a clear, safe, and easy path on which to carry materials to the pond site.

SOIL: Take into account the kind of soil you have, too. It can have a lot to do with whether your installation is easy or difficult. If the soil is especially hard and rocky, save yourself the digging and install an aboveground pond with either flexible or preformed liner supported by a wood, stone, or masonry structure.

Sandy soil comes with problems, too. It is difficult to work with when trying to install an in-ground pond formed from flexible liner, because the sand may cave in along the sides of the pond. Here, a preformed liner may be the answer. To use flexible liner, you'll need to use cinder block under the liner to shore up the sides and hold the edging.

Clay soil, although sometimes difficult to excavate, can be ideal for in-ground installations (and, as you'll see later, for growing water garden plants, too). Clay soil holds its shape, and flexible liner will conform to whatever configuration you dig.

SUN, SHADE, WIND: Take an inventory of the sun and shade patterns in your yard so you can make sure your water garden location will give your plants the sunlight (or the shade) they require. Wind can affect plant life, too. Strong winds speed evaporation from the pond and can break the stems of some tender plants and harm plants that thrive in tranquil water. If you must locate the pond in a wind-prone spot, erect a windscreen, or plant shrubs for a windbreak.

ACCESS: Because existing landscape features such as fences, utility sheds, and other structures can affect access to the pond when you're performing maintenance chores, choose a location that's far enough away from such potential obstacles that you'll have easy access to all sides of the pond. If there's a fence in the vicinity, put your water garden several feet away from it (local codes often specify a distance of 5 feet from a fence).

UTILITIES: Call local utility companies before digging and ask them to locate the lines that run through your property. Most utilities will mark the locations without charge. Even if a utility line is deeper than your pond will be, don't put the pond over an existing line—any future repairs on the line will tear up the pond.

CONSIDER USE

After site conditions, one of the most important aspects to consider when choosing a pond location is how you want to use the pond. Whatever the function and view of your garden pond, make sure it's an integral part of the design, not an add-on. Connect the pond to the perennial bed, the patio, the deck, or other existing features. Study the configuration of the land and tuck your water garden into its contours. Here are some examples of your options.

Will you look out your family room window to see the waterfall? If so, place the waterfall to the back of the pond, facing the window. Add plantings behind it to frame the view.

If your vision of the water garden includes enjoying it while sitting on a deck, you'll want the pond close by, perhaps almost under the deck so it looks like water under a dock. If the deck is elevated, make sure that any waterfall you might have is high enough to be seen over its railing.

If your water garden will be the primary focal point of your entire landscape design, you'll want to situate it so you can take in the entire landscape in one view.

If you want a water garden to fit in with your love of bird-watching, make sure to locate the bird feeders away from and downwind of the pond, to help reduce cleanup problems from hulls and spilled birdseed. A pond that's a natural wildlife setting might fit better in a lesser-used part of the yard, connected to the rest of the landscape with a pebble-surfaced path.

Water gardeners blessed with sloping yards can construct natural-looking streams and waterfalls. Slopes allow for multiple levels to be explored and enjoyed.

Soft, billowy plants at the edge of this pond help it blend seamlessly into the rest of the cottage-style landscape. This type of planting is often referred to as fuzzy edging.

SELECTING A SITE
continued

To integrate the water feature into the rest of the landscape, it helps to use the same or similar elements in the construction of the pond. This pond's edging matches the stone in the patio.

DESIGN ELEMENTS

Water gardens affect the perspective of your landscape and add an element of surprise. Placement of the pond in relation with the rest of your landscape is crucial. If you simply plunk a water garden in the middle of the yard, it will look adrift in a sea of green lawn. Adding a neat row of rocks around its edge just makes matters worse, creating a strangling necklace that looks as though you are trying to hide something.

Think about how the location of the pond can enhance your landscape. For example, a rectangular pond set with its length parallel to the main view from the house will make a yard seem longer. An informal design with the longer sides perpendicular to your line of sight will exaggerate the perspective and make the yard seem larger. Small pools are surprises in the landscape, adding interest for visitors who happen upon them. You can

achieve this sense of delight by tucking a small pond into a side yard or around the bend of a curving flower bed. Add an arbored bench to complete your garden retreat. Whatever you do, integrate the size, scale, and other elements of your water garden with all the features of your landscape.

SIZE: Backyard ponds can be installed in any size, shape, or configuration. Tuck one into a corner of your yard or build the pond so it looks as if it disappears underneath a deck.

Small yards can easily hold a water garden made from nothing more than a large pot or container set into the ground, either partially or completely beneath the soil line. A 2-foot-round hole, overlayed with flexible liner and filled with moist soil, is ideal for a bog garden with a small lotus or a marginal water plant, such as iris or lizard's tail. It provides the perfect opportunity to add water plants to a perennial border when your yard is too small for a full-scale pond.

SCALE: Scale is important when designing a water feature. A large pond can overpower a small landscape. A small water garden in the midst of a large setting can look like a puddle.

There are some tricks that allow you to break the rules of scale. For example, if you would like to build a large pond on a small site, you can create islands, peninsulas, or decks that overhang the pond to break up the visual impact of the water so that it doesn't seem so large. Also, incorporating backgrounds as part of the overall design, as in the photo below, can help give the small element more impact.

Although there are no hard-and-fast rules about the relationship of pond size to yard size, you can estimate the effect of scale with garden hose or colored twine. Lay out the hose or twine in the planned configuration of your pond, and experiment until the scale seems right. Leave the trial outline in place for a week or so to help you decide if the placement of the pond will capitalize on the views from the house, patio, and other spots on your property. This trial run will also help you determine if the water garden fits with the natural traffic patterns in your landscape and whether it will leave enough room for outdoor furniture and decorative objects.

EDGING: Make sure to use an edging that complements other hardscape elements in your overall landscape design. Hardscape elements are those features in your yard that are constructed—decks, arbors, patios, walkways, and driveways, for example. If you've laid a certain type of rock on a path through your perennial bed, use that same rock to edge your water garden. Vary the size of the rocks that you have around the pond so it looks natural and more visually appealing. Similar materials in the pond and overall landscape help achieve a unified, harmonious design.

Using more than one kind of stone in the landscape can be challenging. For instance, if you use mixed fieldstone to edge the perennial bed and flagstone around the pond, either the fieldstone or the flagstone may look out of place. You don't always have to use the same stone, though. A slate patio can be complemented with wood decking or a jagged stone of a similar color. The goal is to harmonize the elements without making one seem out of place or overpowering.

Scale plays an important part in all design. A pond shouldn't overwhelm a site, and the landscape should never feel crowded by the pond. This small pond matches the scale of the small patio. In addition, the wall in the background helps balance their combined "weight."

POND STYLE AND SHAPE

Soft plants combined with irregular stones along the edge enhance this beautiful informal-style pond.

Sharp, straight edges and geometric shapes define formal style. Even wood plank edging can be formal.

Ponds can take whatever shape your imagination and site allow. In terms of style, they break down basically into two categories—formal and informal.

FORMAL STYLE

Clean, simple, straight lines and symmetrical, mirror-image arrangements characterize formal styles. Formal water gardens have straight edges and geometric shapes. Brickwork makes a functional yet highly decorative border for a formal pond, as do square, precast pavers, tile, and even sod.

This geometric pond contains the type of lush, asymmetric plantings usually associated with informal design.

Formal designs work well with manicured beds of roses and neat, evenly planted perennial borders accented with clipped boxwood hedges. If your landscape design is formal and you're considering a reflecting pool—a water feature whose principal function is to reflect trees, the sky, or plantings at the edge of the flower border—square or rectangular shapes are just what you're looking for. For lushness, add a large display of water lilies with a towering papyrus.

INFORMAL STYLE

Curving, fluid lines and asymmetrical arrangements define informal design. The American cottage garden or the mixed perennial border dotted here and there with bright colors provides the perfect setting for an informal pond. An informal water garden flows seamlessly, without defined edges, into the surrounding landscape.

In contrast to formal designs where plants are used as ornament, in informal styles, plants are the heart of the look. Foliage of similar texture and form in both the pond and perennial borders casually links the pond with the rest of the landscape. Edging complements—rather than defines—informal style. Large, irregular fieldstone, river rock, or boulders; logs; or pebbles help make the pond look as if it has always been part of the landscape.

POND SHAPES

Rectangles and squares are typical formal shapes. Because of their straight, simple lines, they work well when you need to define a space, whether the entire garden or part of it.

Oval and circular ponds are difficult to categorize. They may be either formal or informal depending on their size and edging

and the geometry of their plantings. The more a rectangle approaches—but does not become—a circle, the more it will tend to look informal. Soft, planted edges accentuate the effect. A long, narrow, oval pond looks formal, because as its length becomes more than three times its width, it begins to take on the character of a rectangle. It is best to complement it with the hard, formal edges of cut stone or other formal materials.

Free forms, such as crescents and kidney and pie shapes, are informal because of their unsymmetrical edges.

The final shape of your pond is determined by the relationship of its size to its edging. The proportion of plants and edging predominate in a small pond, so these elements influence shape more than the original shape of the hole. You can actually make the right-angled formality of a small rectangular pond disappear by using informal plantings. This is not so with larger ponds. As the size of the excavation increases—to a quarter acre or more, for example—the actual shape becomes predominant.

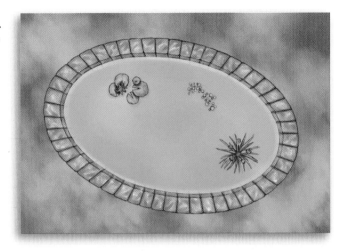

You don't need to build an amoeba-shaped pond to have a free-form design. Plantings dramatically alter the appearance of even the simplest pond shape. Their form, texture, and placement transform the water surface into any shape desired. You can further change the shape of the pond by using stones in a variety of sizes and shapes. In the long run, a pond shaped by plants costs less to build and is easier to maintain than a free-form pond.

FUNCTIONAL MATTERS

Each pond shape requires different quantities of liner and installation time. The more complicated the shape, the more folds you will need to make in the pond liner.

Rectangles are one of the easiest styles to install; you have to make only four folds when using flexible liner, so a rectangle is the most efficient use of flexible materials.

Circular and oval ponds, as well as teardrops and ellipses, are often easier to install when using flexible liner. Because circles and ovals lack corners, the liner is easy to fold.

Free-form designs are the most popular but can also be the most difficult—and the most expensive—to execute because so much liner is taken up in folds and overlaps. These shapes have inner and outer arcs. You'll need to buy enough liner to fit all the outer arcs, which means the inner arcs will have too much liner in them and you'll have to take it up. A crescent-shaped pond can require one-third more liner than a rectangular one of equivalent size; a pie-shaped pond requires less liner than a crescent of the same area. In small ponds, this extra amount isn't critical, but it's a nightmare in large ponds.

AMOEBA PONDS

Avoid shapes that exhibit the "amoeba syndrome"—those that have "lobes" extending from the main body of the design. Lobes mean pinches, and pinches mean folds and extra liner. These shapes will drive you crazy when you try to install them with all the folding they require. What's more, the lobes create dead zones in the pond where water can't easily circulate. Pond water settles into these dead areas and reduces oxygen levels, which is not good for fish or fauna. Once the garden matures, the pond loses its artistic, free-form shape. On top of all this, the pond lobes are difficult to mow around.

FORM, TEXTURE, AND COLOR

Plantings around the pond are just as important as the shape of the pond. Their form gives vertical structure to the water; their texture provides a rich canvas on which to work.

Bushy, upright form: umbrella grass

Upright form: iris

Bold and bushy form: melon sword

Creeping form: moneywort

Plants bring glory to a backyard water feature, transforming a pond from a sterile, flat plane of water into a living, breathing world added to your landscape. It is often the choice of plants more than pool shape and edging that creates the feel and flavor of the water garden. Plants add height, texture, and dimension, making the pond a true garden oasis.

Plant form and texture are two of the primary elements in water garden design. Along with color, they bring balance and mood to the garden that can be only hinted at by its hardscape. They are the elements that give the garden dimension.

FORM

Form means the overall shape of the plant. Generally speaking, a plant's form may be upright, mounding (sometimes called bushy), or creeping. Upright plants are tall and columnar. They give vertical thrust to the landscape, as does a fountain or an upright stone. Mounding plants are lower and rounded. Their shape ties the form of upright plants to the landscape, anchoring the vertical plants to the design. Creeping plants lie lower to the ground; in the pond, they float on the surface. Their creeping, horizontal habit directs our eyes through the design, forward, backward, and side to side.

Well-balanced water garden designs include a harmonious blend of vertical, mounding, and creeping plants. A design that uses only one kind of plant form is one-dimensional and less inviting. For example, if you compose your garden solely of upright plants, it may look top-heavy and uninteresting. Similarly, a

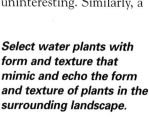

Select water plants with form and texture that mimic and echo the form and texture of plants in the surrounding landscape.

Fine texture: corkscrew rush

pond that lacks transitions from the taller plants to the ground—one that has no mounding plants—may appear abrupt, as if something has been left out.

For example, umbrella grass is an attractive upright plant that gives height to a design. Melon sword (*Echinodorus cordifolius*) is shorter and more rounded in habit. Combining these plants with a creeper, such as water hyssop, makes an attractive, three-tiered planting at the edge of the pond.

TEXTURE

Plant texture is another element of water garden design that will make your garden vibrant. Texture is defined as fine, medium, and coarse, terms that are applied to plant foliage and other elements in the design.

Fine texture is often associated with pine trees and needled evergreens. Fine-textured plants have thin or tiny leaves, about the size of pebbles. The leaves on a medium-textured plant are about the size of a serving spoon or the width of a butter knife. Coarse foliage is large and bold, ranging from the size of a hockey puck to a beach ball; some hardy plants with coarse foliage almost look tropical.

Even the tiniest container pond benefits from a mixture of plant forms and textures. By combining plant texture and form, you'll have a richer palette to work with. Plants on the water surface generally are limited to representing the horizontal aspect of design. It's on the margin of your pond that you have the greatest opportunity for varying plant form and texture.

You'll find that your garden will be even more exciting if you rely on elements other than plants to provide the design features. Borrow from the hardscaping. Use edging as the horizontal element along with creeping plants. A large, round boulder can stand in for a bushy plant, a tall stone for an upright

plant. Combining stones and hardscape with the plants adds yet more character and depth. Soften a large boulder by underplanting it with yellow flag iris and parrot's feather. Pebbles at the edge of the pond take on more vibrant character when they serve as the footing for a bold planting of corkscrew rush or 'Black Magic' taro.

COLOR

The colors of the water garden may be as muted or as loud as those of any perennial border. You can use them to create themes, set moods, or awaken the senses. Because the pond landscape should reflect the sensibilities of the gardener who built it, choose colors you like or that have meaning for you.

Select all-white flowers contrasted with plants of all-blue foliage to have your own moon garden. White flowers will also light up a shady corner of the pond. Blues and greens create a cool, relaxing atmosphere. Soft, pastel shades create a pond reminiscent of a Monet painting.

A simple water garden in a terra-cotta pot is stunning when planted with the bright orange flowers and striking yellow and green foliage of 'Praetoria' canna, complemented by the bright blue flowers and shiny green leaves of lemon bacopa.

Coarse or bold texture: gunnera

Coarse or bold texture: taro

Coarse or bold texture: canna

Medium texture: lizard's tail

Medium texture: lobelia

Plant shapes vary from narrowly upright to arching to rounded to flat. Here, the upright form of the iris accents the arching ornamental grass in the background.

COLOR AND SEASONAL CHANGES

Just as daffodils trumpet the arrival of spring in a perennial garden, so too does the pond have its own harbingers. Even if the water is still cold, the pond can be full of life and color.

The water garden reflects the changing moods of the seasons, just as the perennial border and the rest of the landscape do. Each season—spring through summer and fall through winter—impresses its own distinctive personality on the pond.

SPRING

The water garden's harbinger of spring is the marsh marigold. Its common name speaks to its resemblance to its dryland namesake. This marginal plant has waxy, bright yellow flowers and mounds of shiny, rounded, serrated leaves. Marsh marigolds peek their heads above the ice-crusted soil at the edge of the pond in early spring, about the same time that crocuses begin to appear in the perennial border. Like crocus, marsh marigold pays no heed to cold winds or falling snow.

Color in the spring pond is apparent not only in early blooms but also in the new foliage that starts to sprout along the margins of the pond and in bog gardens beside it. Blue flag pushes up its new leaves—pointed swords of green that are streaked with beet red or deep purple at the base. These add important color to the pond when little else in the yard has yet to awake. Blue rushes, with their

almost ever-blue foliage, add still more color to the edge of the spring water garden, as do early-rising sweet flags and sedge, which jump-start the summer color season by two to three months.

On the water surface itself, water hawthorn emerges early, as the ice is leaving the pond, producing fragrant, floating, white flowers. Water lilies are barely waking up, but white water buttercup (*Ranunculus longirostris*) and floating marsh marigold (*Caltha natans*) will soon be showing their dainty flowers on the water surface. Pink blush tinges the foliage of early-emerging marginals, including 'Flamingo' rainbow water parsley, variegated manna grass, and 'Candy Stripe' reed.

Marsh marigold and skunk cabbage are an unbeatable combination in a spring bog or pond.

In summer, the pond is at its peak. The perennial garden may be waning, but the water garden bursts with blooms. Water lilies and lotus bask in the summer sun like bathers at the beach.

SUMMER

As spring gives way to summer, marsh marigold and hyacinth lose their blush, but color continues to burst forth in the water garden. Irises bloom along the margins, and water lilies and water snowflakes flower on the surface of the water, beginning an early-summer show that lasts until the fall frost.

Just as you would check your perennial border, check your water garden week by week. Don't fall into the water-lily trap and look only for marginals with color when the water lilies are not in bloom, then forget all about marginals once the water lilies start to flower. If you have any holes or gaps when nothing is in bloom on the water surface, take a look around your local water garden supplier to see what is in bloom.

Fill in empty spots to keep the design in balance. Tropical marginals, such as cannas and white-topped sedge, can be useful in providing early-summer color. Their bright, vibrant flowers and lush foliage bridge the spring and summer seasons, and they continue to flower right until frost.

July and August are the months when the water garden is truly at its peak. Lotus begin to flower in July. Pickerel weed is in full flush in summer months, when water lilies also reach their full potential. Even on scorching summer days when the perennial garden looks peaked, the water garden thrives and flourishes in the heat and humidity.

FALL

Once fall arrives, the water garden still has something to offer. Although most water plants turn to mush after the first frost or have little autumnal color other than brown,

some wait for the cooler months to put on their best show. These include sedges and blue rushes, which take on a purple hue after a frost. It's as though they were waiting all summer for their chance to really shine.

European bugleweed (*Lycopus europaeus*) offers a dazzling display of purple, as does frog fruit. Star fruit (*Penthorum sedoides*) becomes the burning bush of the pond, with fiery oranges, reds, pinks, and yellows. Tufts-of-gold (*Lysimachia thyrsiflora*) is ablaze with golden-yellow foliage and pinkish-red stems. Cattails, willows, and red-stemmed dogwoods (*Cornus stolonifera* or *C. sericea*) add to the backdrop.

WINTER

Winter, although the bleakest of seasons, can still hold interest. Blue rushes as well as corkscrew rushes are almost evergreen— or ever-blue— even in snow. Water parsnip (*Sium suave*) and water dock (*Rumex hydrolapathum*) stand tall, their seed heads offering birds a welcome treat. Like those of soft rush, their seed heads, as well as the catkins of the cattail, catch the snow as it falls softly to the ground, and their chocolate-brown stems stand out in contrast to the white of the snow, like sentinels keeping watch over the pond until spring.

Lobelias, such as this 'Sparkle Divine', take the water garden into fall, adding colorful blossoms.

PLANTS FOR THE WATER GARDEN

A landscape feature with rocks, fountains, and clear, glittering water dresses up any yard. Without plants, though, it may look something like a glorified swimming pool. Add water plants to the design and you will see a complete transformation.

Plants soften the landscape, making it a place of true beauty, a lush and green respite from the hard, gray workaday world of concrete and asphalt. Plants tie the pond to the rest of the landscape by providing a colorful and textured transition from the pond to the yard.

Plants are functional as well as beautiful. Large pots brimming with plants conceal the hard edge of a preformed pond, so that the pond looks natural in its surroundings. Plants growing in and around the water provide safe haven for frogs, toads, and other amphibians, too. In the water, plants supply cover and shade for koi and goldfish. Marginal plants attract birds and butterflies, even hummingbirds. Other plants aid in the biological stability of the pond, adding oxygen to the water and consuming harmful or algae-feeding nutrients in the water, removing them from the pond.

Water lilies, floating plants, parrot's feather, and other marginals all come together to blend the pond into the garden and add life to the landscape.

Mail-order and local nurseries, pond shops, garden centers, and even some home improvement stores carry plants and the supplies needed for their care.

Aquatic plants are easy to grow. Simply pot them up and put them in water. Some don't even need a pot.

A WEALTH OF PLANT CHOICES

There are water plants to fit every need and every budget. In a tiny water garden, a single water lily with a few marginal plants, such as a dwarf arrowhead and a Japanese sweet flag, provide color and interest all summer long. Just one water lily will produce flowers from the time the water warms until frost, adding color and charm to even a small container pond. So will just a few inexpensive floating plants.

Snowflakes and other water-lily-like plants are even less costly. Marginal water plants, which grow with their roots in wet soil while most of their foliage stands out of the water, come in all shapes, colors, and sizes.

Medium-sized ponds can use taller, more substantial marginals, such as pickerel weed and soft rush. In very large ponds, very large marginals are appropriate, such as papyrus, which reaches up to 9 feet in height. Large pots of water lilies and submerged plants help fill out a pond.

Water-loving plants are easy to care for and are not usually bothered by pests or diseases. They grow readily in average garden soil and need only a monthly dose of fertilizer in spring and summer. Those that are winter-hardy may be left in the pond during the cold months. Frost-tender selections can be brought indoors to overwinter as houseplants with their pots in a saucer of water.

YOUR GUIDE

This chapter guides you through the many types of water garden plants and helps you select the ones that speak to your heart as well as your budget. It will also guide you in growing and caring for the plants.

Tropical water lilies, such as this 'Director George T. Moore', provide fragrance and sparkle in the water garden. Their shades of blue and purple are completely absent in hardy lilies.

WHAT ARE WATER PLANTS?

Water plants come in all shapes and sizes. Some grow completely underwater; others only want their toes wet. Depending on how and where they grow in the pond, water garden plants fall into six categories. You'll find general descriptions of each category below and information about specific species, varieties and cultivars on the pages that follow.

Each is accompanied by planting tips, including the amount of sunlight and shade needed, the hardiness of the plant, its stem length and spread, and water depth (the distance from the water surface to the crown of the plant). By way of explanation, "part shade" means four to six hours of sunlight daily or constant dappled shade. Also, a "running" plant grows in one or two directions, like a vine; a plant with a "creeping" habit grows equally in all directions.

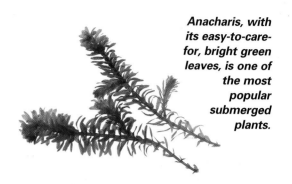

Anacharis, with its easy-to-care-for, bright green leaves, is one of the most popular submerged plants.

just above the water surface during the summer. Although most plants add a small amount of oxygen to the water, submerged plants do so more effectively. If you look closely, you can see bubbles forming on their leaves. In addition, submerged plants remove nutrients from water, which helps to contain algae growth. Most submerged plants thrive in water depths of up to 10 feet, but some varieties need only a little light and grow at depths of 15 to 30 feet.

Water plants fall into six categories, and this scene showcases four of them: lotus, marginals (sedge and thalia), water lilies, and oxygenators.

In each of the six categories are plants called filtrators. Filtrators absorb large amounts of nutrients, readily soaking them up from the water and keeping them from algae. They reduce nitrogen levels in the water, which is conducive to healthy fish life.

SUBMERGED PLANTS AND OXYGENATORS

Aquatics whose foliage grows entirely underwater are called submerged water plants. Just because their leaves don't rise above the surface of the water doesn't mean they're not beautiful. Many submerged plants have colorful foliage that glistens underwater, and several even have flowers that float on or rise

FLOATING WATER PLANTS

Plants that sit on the water surface with no need of pot or soil are called floating water plants. Their roots dangle in the water, drawing from the pond nitrogen and phosphates that could otherwise cause an algae bloom.

Floaters are extremely easy to grow—you can even grow them in a watertight pot on your deck or patio. Some flower with bright blue blooms that start when the weather warms and continue until fall. Although some floating plants are winter-hardy, most are not. But they are among the cheapest of all water plants, so treat them as annuals and buy them fresh each year. In winter, simply pull them out of the pond and add them to the compost pile. Because of their high nitrogen content, they'll add nutrients to the pile.

WATER LILIES

Like marginals, water lilies grow with their roots and stems in soil below the water surface, but their foliage—round leaves that look like green platters—floats on the water. Some cultivars also have floating flowers; others hold their blooms on stems several inches out of the water. Most water lilies grow in 3- to 4-foot depths, some in depths of up to 8 feet, but they do quite well in ponds with only 6 to 18 inches of water over their roots. They provide shade and cover for fish, as well as an egg-laying platform for certain species of dragonflies whose larvae feed on insects.

Water lilies are classified into two broad groups. Hardy water lilies survive winters in cold climates. Tropical water lilies cannot withstand a winter freeze and need special care during cold months. To tell if a water lily is hardy or tropical, look at the edge of its rounded leaves. If the edge is smooth, the lily is hardy. If the edge is crinkled, wavy, or toothed, the lily is tropical.

HARDY WATER LILIES: Flowers come in many colors, and some even change their color each day of their three-day bloom life. Hardy water lilies flower during the day, with blossoms opening around 9 a.m. and closing around 4 p.m.

TROPICAL WATER LILIES: There are day-blooming cultivars and night bloomers. Like their hardy counterparts, the flowers of the day-bloomers open around 9 a.m. and close about 4 p.m. Night-blooming tropicals open after the sun sets and stay open the next morning until sometime between 10 and 12.

Tropical water lilies have a distinct, enticing fragrance that floats on the wind, often announcing from several feet away that the flowers are open. Most hardy water lilies are not nearly as fragrant.

MARGINALS

At the edge, or margin, of the pond, where the soil is moist or the water shallow, grow the "marginals." These plants have their roots in soil and most of their foliage out of the water. Some grow in soil that is only moist or wet; others grow in submerged soil—from a few inches to about 2 feet. Many marginals will also adapt to the perennial garden, as long as the soil is kept fairly moist. This adaptability makes them ideal as transitional plants that link the pond with other gardens.

Marginals can be taller than 6 feet or less than 2 inches in height. Some are clump-forming, such as hosta, and stay where they're put. Others are rambling types that traverse the pond edge. Their chief function is decorative, adding color, texture, and form to the design. They're also an important transitional element in the landscape.

WATER-LILY-LIKE PLANTS

These plants grow in soil from 1 inch to 2 feet below the water surface; like water lilies, they hold their leaves and flowers on top of the water. Although they grow like water lilies, botanically they are not, and so they are in a separate group. Some, such as water hawthorn, are very winter-hardy. (Water hawthorn prefers the cool waters of spring and fall to summer's heat and may go dormant in hot weather). The small form and plentiful blooming of water-lily-like plants make them an excellent choice for container gardens and provides delicate contrast to other pond plants.

LOTUSES

Lotuses are similar to water lilies, growing in wet soil in water up to 3 feet deep, but unlike water lilies, they hold some of their leaves and all of their flowers well above the water. In modern cultivars, the blooms rise well above the leaves. Lotus leaves are round and either float or stand out of the water like inverted parasols. They have a waxy covering that makes raindrops roll around like little balls of mercury. Lotus provide cover for fish and aquatic animals and food for nectar-seeking insects.

Lotus cultivars grow from 6 inches to 6 feet in height. Smaller selections, called bowl lotus, can live happily in containers less than a foot wide and in just a few inches of soil and water. Lotus plants also grow well in bog gardens with a few inches of water.

Use as many of the six kinds of water plants as possible for an appealing pond that's less likely to suffer water-quality or algae problems. Plants from four of the groups fill this water garden.

Lotus, planted here among blue pickerel weed, grows well in containers or on the boggy edge of a pond.

Water-lily-like water snowflakes shade the pond and provide cover for fish in hot weather.

SUBMERGED PLANTS

Important to water quality as well as clarity, the underwater foliage of submerged plants (also called oxygenators) filters unwanted nutrients. During the day, the plants add oxygen to the water, and at night they remove it. Too many submerged plants, however, can cause wide pH swings, so in a pond with fish, keep their area to about half the size of the pond. The time to plant most oxygenators is when water temperatures reach 55° to 60° F.

Looking something like an underwater juniper bush, hornwort is a many-branched oxygenator with thick, dense, dark green foliage. It grows in a fluffy mat that floats just below the surface; because it doesn't produce roots, there's no need for pot or soil—just put it in the pond. If you want to keep it in one location and at a certain depth, rubber-band it to a brick. It makes an excellent spawning ground for fish in spring and is somewhat resistant to koi feeding.

Clockwise from left: anacharis, pondweed, and fanwort

EGERIA DENSA
Anacharis

- Sun to shade
- Zones 8 to 11
- Stem length: to 10 feet
- Spread: 1 foot
- Water depth: 1 to 10 feet

Anacharis has shiny, fleshy, bright green leaves that radiate from a central stem; it resembles submerged feather dusters. Three-petaled white flowers float on the water surface in summer. To overwinter anacharis in cold climates, bring in stem cuttings and keep them in an aquarium, where they will quickly root and grow.

CABOMBA CAROLINIANA
Fanwort

- Sun to shade
- Zones 5 to 11
- Stem length: to 6 feet
- Spread: 1 foot
- Water depth: 1 to 10 feet

A submerged aquatic with delicate and finely cut foliage (dark green above, deep purple underneath), fanwort is winter-hardy, even in cold regions where ice forms on the pond. In summer, it grows long stems that reach to the water surface and sprouts a multitude of small white flowers with bright yellow centers. An attractive aquatic in the backyard pond, it has a fluffy structure that is excellent for goldfish spawning.

CERATOPHYLLUM DEMERSUM
Hornwort

- Sun to part shade
- Zones 5 to 11
- Stem length: to 10 feet
- Spread: 1 foot or more
- Water depth: 1 to 10 feet

ELODEA CANADENSIS
Common Elodea

- Best in full sun
- Zones 3 to 9
- Stem length: to 6 feet
- Spread: 12 inches
- Water depth: 6 inches to 40 feet, as deep as the light is sufficient

This plant likes water that is fairly cool (65° to 75° F) and alkaline. It does best in fine sand with a small amount (about 20 percent) of peat moss. Propagate it from stem cuttings. Its dwarf habit and hardiness make it excellent for small ponds in northern regions,

Elodea

Hornwort

and it's a favored food of koi and goldfish. It is rather brittle so it is not suitable for water gardens that have fish a foot or more in length (unless you plant a lot of it). Some studies report that it secretes a chemical compound that reduces mosquito larva populations by 30 percent.

FONTINALIS ANTIPYRETICA
Willow Moss

- Full shade
- Zones 3 to 11, depending on species
- Height: floating to just below the surface
- Spread: creeping
- Water depth: to 18 inches

This free-floating plant is the ultimate spawning media—soft and covered with small, scalelike leaves to which eggs easily adhere. Willow moss requires fairly clean, soft, and neutral to slightly acidic water, so if it fails to thrive, your water needs attention.

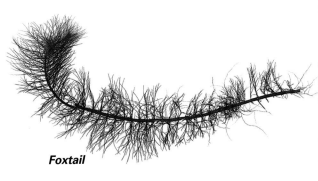

Foxtail

MYRIOPHYLLUM HETEROPHYLLUM
Foxtail

- Sun to shade
- Zones 3 to 11
- Stem length: to 6 feet
- Spread: 1 foot
- Water depth: 1 to 10 feet

A very winter-hardy underwater favorite, this plant has thin, wispy leaves that grow from a stout central stem. Foliage is dark reddish brown and fluffy when submerged, somewhat like a fox's tail, from which it derives its common name. There are several similar species including M. *hippuroides*, and M. *spicata*. M. *spicata* is often sold, but it is highly invasive.

POTAMOGETON CRISPUS
Curled Pondweed

- Sun to part shade
- Zones 4 to 11
- Stem length: to 3 feet
- Spread: running
- Water depth: 10 feet

One of many species of pondweed native to North America, curled pondweed has leaves that are long and wavy, with edges like crinkly red aluminum foil. This plant is an important source of food for waterfowl, and its submerged leaves make a good spawning ground for fish.

Curled pondweed

RANUNCULUS LONGIROSTRIS
Water Buttercup

- Sun or part shade
- Zones 4 to 11
- Stem length: to 4 feet
- Spread: 1 foot
- Water depth: 1 to 6 feet

The leaves of this plant are very finely cut, open and airy, and almost threadlike, borne alternately radiating from a central stem. Like fanwort, water buttercup has large white flowers in summer that float on the water surface. It is more brittle than fanwort, and its stems can break easily when handled. In still or slow-moving water (which it prefers), it can form dense stands. It is an excellent early filtrator (plant it in 35° F water) and starts growing early in spring. Yellow water crowfoot (R. *flabellaris*) has flat leaves, and its June-blooming flowers are yellow.

White water buttercup

NOTE

A few of these submerged plants have become noxious weeds in some areas, clogging natural waterways. Before buying plants, check with the local department of natural resources to make sure the plants have not been banned in your state. Even though your water garden may be miles from a natural body of water, birds and other critters can transport seeds and start an infestation.

SUBMERGED PLANTS
continued

Dwarf arrowhead on the left; normal-sized S. natans on the right

SAGITTARIA NATANS
Arrowhead

- Sun to shade
- Zones 4 to 11
- Stem length: to 3 feet
- Spread: 6 inches to creeping
- Water depth: 2 to 3 feet for flowering; it will grow deeper but may not flower

Looking much like eel grass but with thicker leaves, this plant is not as fluid in the water, but it is sturdy enough to hold up to koi and large goldfish. It is one of the first plants up in spring, so it is a great aid in removing fish waste. Displaying the largest blossoms of any of the submerged plants listed here, it has white summer flowers, held on the water surface, which are up to half an inch in diameter. Plants spread by creeping stolons to form sods or colonies. Dwarf arrowhead (*S. subulata*) forms a submerged, 4- to 6-inch sod and is ideal for small ponds. Plant arrowhead in 4 to 12 inches of water, and in summer you will have white flowers floating on the surface. In deeper water, it may never flower, but its extra surface will aid in filtration. In an earth-bottom pond, plant it in a shallow tray topped off with pea gravel so the fish won't dig it up.

Bladderwort

UTRICULARIA VULGARIS
Bladderwort

- Sun to shade
- Zones 3 to 11
- Stem length: 2 to 24 inches, depending on species

- Spread: 1 to 6 inches, depending on species
- Water depth: floats just below the surface

An unusual submerged plant for the pond or the aquarium (it's carnivorous), bladderwort has very fine foliage. Some plants look like soft hornwort. Others are so fine that they look like floating bits of green hairnet or string algae; they provide food and cover for fish. Nestled among the foliage are tiny "bladders," which trap microscopic prey. Leaves and stems grow as floating mats just below the water surface. Their dainty yellow, white, purple, or lavender blossoms stand above the water surface and resemble small snapdragons. Most bladderworts prefer neutral to acidic water conditions. Because they do not produce roots, no soil or potting is necessary.

VALLISNERIA SPIRALIS
Eel Grass

- Sun to shade
- Zones 4 to 11
- Stem length: 2 to 3 feet
- Spread: running
- Water depth: 1 to 15 feet

The plants in this genus of several species of submerged plants have long, tapelike leaves. Their foliage often ripples in moving water—excellent near the base of a waterfall or in deep streams. Selections come in a variety of colors and shapes, with both red-leaved and twisted or curled foliage. Plants grow from underground runners to form large colonies in earth-bottom ponds that are ideal for small fish to hide. 'Crystal' eel grass has a green, glassy look. 'Red Jungle' eel grass has broad burgundy foliage.

Left to right clockwise: 'Red Jungle', 'Curly', and 'American' eel grass

FLOATING AND WATER-LILY-LIKE PLANTS

Floating water plants are the ultimate in easy gardening—there's no potting necessary. Just set them in the water. Because they float on the water surface, floaters grow in any depth of water. They are among the best filtrators. They shade fish from sun and protect them from predators. Too many floaters in a pond, however, can reduce oxygen, which harms fish. Don't let floaters completely cover the pond's surface.

AZOLLA CAROLINIANA
Fairy Moss

- Sun to shade
- Zones 9 to 11
- Height: floating
- Spread: running

This fern, its leaves fuzzy and finely toothed, is bright green in summer, red in spring and fall. An excellent cover for fish and other wildlife, it can be planted just after the ice is off. Fairy moss is light-sensitive and tends to die during the short days of winter. It fixes its own nitrogen, which will enrich the compost pile later on. *A. pinnata*, invasive and prohibited under federal law, has triangular leaves.

CERATOPTERIS THALICTROIDES
Water Fern

- Part to full shade, does not tolerate sun
- Zones 9 to 11
- Height: 1 foot
- Spread: running

The foliage of this unusual plant looks like big, puffy parsley. New plantlets form on the leaves. Water fern grows floating on water and in soil with a few inches of water over its crown. In soil, it looks like curly parsley. The foliage of *C. pteridoides* is slightly coarser in appearance. Plant water fern when water reaches 65° F.

EICHHORNIA CRASSIPES
Water Hyacinth

- Sun to part shade
- Zones 9 to 11
- Height: to 1 foot
- Spread: running

Known for its lavender flowers and shiny, round, spongy, green foliage, this floater filters so well that it is sometimes grown to treat sewage.

It does best in warm water, and won't survive freezing weather. Wait until the water is consistently above 65° F before planting. In cold climates, treat it like an annual.

Water hyacinth makes an ideal container plant. Drop it in any pot that holds water and add fertilizer. Creeping or peacock water hyacinth (*E. azurea*) grows from a thick, fleshy stem that spreads across the water surface. Its blue flowers are smaller and more rounded. It is illegal to possess water hyacinth in some states, and federal law prohibits interstate commerce of it.

From upper left: 'Aqua Velvet', 'Ruffles', and regular water lettuce; frogbit (round leaves); salvinia (rectangular leaves); duckweed (light green); water hyacinth; and azolla (dark green in center).

HYDROCHARIS MORSUS-RANAE AND LIMNOBIUM SPONGIA
Frogbit

- Sun to part shade
- Zones 4 to 10
- Height: floating to ½ inch tall
- Spread: running

The common name frogbit actually refers to several different plants. *Hydrocharis morsus-ranae* is the prettiest, with small, three-petaled, white summer flowers like miniature water poppies. The foliage is shiny and heart-shaped. This plant grows well in small ponds and containers. In winter, its buds sink to the bottom of the pond, where it overwinters until spring. American frogbit (*Limnobium spongia*), a look-alike with oval leaves, has not-very-showy, quarter-inch blossoms. In most climates, you'll find frogbit available for planting in late April.

FLOATING AND WATER-LILY-LIKE PLANTS
continued

*Left to right:
Marsh marigold,
water hawthorn,
Illinois pondweed,
and water clover
(see page 40)*

LEMNA MINOR
Duckweed

- Sun to part shade
- Zones 3 to 11
- Height: floating
- Spread: running

Known as the smallest flowering plant in the world, common duckweed has round or almost-round light green leaves less than ⅛ inch in diameter, with a single root growing from under the leaf. Duckweed is a favorite of goldfish and koi. Use it as a spring and fall fish food, planting just after the ice leaves the pond. Caution: Duckweed can overtake a pond in a single season unless checked by fish or judicious thinning.

PISTIA STRATIOTES
Water Lettuce

- Sun to part shade
- Zones 9 to 11
- Height: 4 to 12 inches
- Spread: running (up to a foot wide)

Its spongy, velvety, lime green foliage grows like a rosette from a single crown, resembling

a floating head of lettuce. 'Ruffles' (4 to 6 inches in diameter) has smaller leaves with folds obscuring the center. 'Aqua Velvet' (6 to 8 inches wide) has deep blue-green leaves. 'Angio Splash' (6 to 8 inches across) is streaked and blotched in creamy yellow. Plant when the water is 65° F.

SALVINIA LONGIFOLIA
Salvinia

- Sun to part shade
- Zones 10 and 11
- Height: floating
- Spread: running

Like fairy moss, salvinia is a true fern. The species has velvety leaves that grow on a long, floating chain. *S. longifolia*, good food for small fish but aggressive in southern climates, has 1- to 3-inch, oval leaves and should be used only in northern areas; it's excellent in containers or small ponds where control is easier. *S. molesta*, invasive and prohibited in many southern states, has round leaves. In northern climates it is very cold-sensitive, requiring a minimum water temperature of 40° F before planting.

WATER-LILY-LIKE PLANTS

Water lilies aren't the only plants that grow from a submerged crown with floating leaves and flowers. Other aquatics have adapted to water in the same way, and some are winter-hardy enough to stay in the pond all year. Keep the tender ones indoors in an aquarium in a sunny window during winter months. Their small foliage and blossoms provide an unusual accent to water lilies in any size pond.

APONOGETON DISTACHYUS (SYN. A. DISTACHYOS)
Water Hawthorn

- Sun to part shade
- Zones 5 to 11
- Spread: 2 feet
- Water depth: 6 to 24 inches

Ornamental and extremely fragrant, water hawthorn smells like vanilla. Blooms appear when the water is just above freezing, in spring and again in fall. In cold, spring-fed waters, it can blossom all year. In warm water, it may go completely dormant in summer. Propagate it whenever the plants produce bulblike seeds. Push the seeds into the soil, so their tips just show.

CALTHA NATANS
Floating Marsh Marigold

- Sun to part shade
- Zones 2 to 7
- Spread: 1 foot
- Water depth: 2 to 6 inches

Floating marsh marigold is a dainty, spring-flowering plant for tub gardens and small ponds. Its white, single-petaled blossoms, only as big as a quarter, appear when the ice is off the pond. Its heart-shaped leaves are also very small. Floating marsh marigold will die if not kept in water cooler than 65° F.

HYDROCLEYS NYMPHOIDES
Water Poppy

- Sun to part shade
- Zones 9 to 11
- Spread: to 6 feet
- Water depth: 4 to 12 inches

This tender aquatic has rounded, slightly inflated leaves and creamy, 2-inch, yellow flowers with dark red or brown stamens. It starts blooming in 75° F water and keeps going all summer. Giant water poppy (*H. peruviana*) is about half again as large as the standard water poppy but is otherwise identical. Water poppy sprouts new floating plantlets that flower and grow more leaves and stems across the water surface. It is considered a nuisance in warm climates, where it can quickly take over a pond. Divide it by breaking off the floating stems after they have rooted. You can

Left to right: Water poppy, Peruvian water poppy

also grow it from seed when the water temperature reaches 70° F.

NYMPHOIDES
Water Snowflakes

- Sun to part shade
- Zones 7 to 11
- Spread: running
- Water depth: 4 to 24 inches

Most water-lily-like plants that fall into the snowflake family have dainty white or yellow flowers that often rise from the junction of a leaf on the same stem. *N. aquatica*, also called banana plant, has tubers that in the aquarium look like little bunches of green bananas. In the water garden, it has floating, round leaves and diminutive white flowers shaped like a star. Painted yellow water snowflake (*N. crenata*) has toothed leaves heavily mottled in dark red. Flowers are yellow, star-shaped, and fringed. Painted white water snowflake (*N. cristata*) has leaves heavily painted in dark burgundy and white, star-shaped, lightly fringed flowers. Yellow water snowflake (*N. geminata*, syn. *N. peltata*) has foliage that's an even green, not mottled or variegated; flowers are yellow, star-shaped, and frilly. Free-flowering and fast-growing and hardy in cold climates, it will overwinter in Zones 5 to 11. White water snowflake (*N. indica*) is just like yellow water snowflake except it has white, star-shaped, frilly flowers. 'Gigantea' has flowers larger than the species. Orange water snowflake (*N. hydrocharioides*) has fringed orange flowers and slightly mottled leaves. It is otherwise similar to white water snowflake. Plant when the water temperature is above 70° F.

Left to right: Painted white water snowflake, white water snowflake, yellow water snowflake

POTAMOGETON ILLINOENSIS
Illinois Pondweed

- Sun to shade
- Zones 3 to 9
- Spread: to 3 feet
- Water depth: 1 to 15 feet

Illinois pondweed is one of several species of *Potamogeton*. It has elliptical, shiny, khaki green leaves. Its late-summer flowers are clublike and rise a few inches out of the water. You can plant it just after the pond has thawed.

WATER LILIES

Some water lilies are small enough to fit in a fish bowl, others so large they can cover a pond. Flower colors of hardy water lilies fall on the red side of the spectrum.

Water lilies are often considered the jewels of the pond. We can visualize a pond without marginals or submerged plants, even without fish. Who can imagine one without water lilies?

Water lilies belong to the genus *Nymphaea*, but virtually all the lilies available today are named cultivars that have been hybridized by cross-fertilization. Native species are not the best for the homeowner's pond, because they are not as ornamental and do not perform as reliably as named cultivars.

'Red Flare' is a night-blooming tropical whose mahogany leaves add an extra dimension to the pond.

There is even a "changeable" group of hardy water lilies whose blossoms open one color, then age to a different hue. These are good for the small pond or container that holds only one or two lilies.

Many dark red selections are more suitable to northern climates. In very warm areas, their petals may "melt" in the afternoon summer sun. However, newer selections have been developed to avoid this. One cultivar, 'Almost Black', has dark red flowers the color of dark cherry soda.

Water lilies are often classified by their leaf spread—that is, how much water surface the plant will cover once it is mature. Hardy water lilies can have a spread anywhere from 1 to 8 feet in diameter. The largest lilies, such as 'Gladstone' (also called 'Gladstoniana') are particularly suitable for large water gardens and earth-bottom ponds and will grow well in water 1 to 4 feet deep. The smallest, called miniatures, have flowers only 1 to 2 inches wide.

The white-flowering pygmy water lily, *N. tetragona*, blooms earliest, in the cool waters of spring. Soon to follow are the pink forms, 'Joanne Pring' and 'Rosea Laydekeri'. Last to appear are the bright yellow blossoms of 'Helvola'.

Hardy water lilies also differ with respect to the growth habit of their rootstocks, which can affect how you use the plants, how much attention they need, and how they perform in your pond.

Odorata types and tuberosa types grow with rhizomes horizontally across the soil surface. Both types can grow wild and unrestrained, requiring more frequent division to contain them in their pots. (Odorata lily

HARDY WATER LILIES

- Full sun (some cultivars bloom even in part shade)
- Zones 3 to 11
- Spread: 1 to 8 feet, depending on cultivar
- Height: floating
- Water depth: 6 to 36 inches; some varieties tolerate deeper water, even up to 8 feet
- Flowers: when pond water is over 65° F

HARDY WATER LILIES

Hardy water lilies are day bloomers. They open around 9 a.m. and close around 4 p.m. On dark, cloudy days, they may not open at all. Generally, their flowers rest on the water surface. Hardy water lily cultivars flower in a wide range of colors, from the darkest reds to the purest whites, with bright pinks and creamy yellows in between. The only colors missing are blues and purples.

Although there has never been a true orange water lily, recent introductions include several peach-flowering hardy water lilies. 'Barbara Dobbins' has flowers the color of cantaloupe, with big goblet-sized blossoms that rise up out of the water; 'Colorado' has salmon-colored flowers, with large, pointed petals.

'Mayla', large, hardy lily

rhizomes can be larger than 3 inches in diameter and can spread more than 3 feet in a single year.)

Because these types put more energy into tuber and leaf production than into blossoms, they tend not to flower as often as the modern hybrids. The tuberosas are more productive than odoratas.

Two other types, Marliac and Mexicana, exhibit more restrained root growth and better flower and foliage production in a smaller space.

Marliac-type water lilies have more compact roots and do not run across the soil as much as odorata and tuberosa types. They are named after Joseph Bory Latour-Marliac of the village Temple sur Lot in France. In the late 1800s and early 1900s, Marliac hybridized many of the hundreds of hardy water lily cultivars so popular today.

'Pink Pearl', tropical, day blooming

Mexicana-type water lilies have upright, nonrunning rhizomes and are named after the semihardy *N. mexicana* water lily, which has this type of rhizome. The rhizome shape is similar to a small pineapple, which it is also sometimes called. Many of the changeable water lilies and 'Chromatella' have Mexicana-type rhizomes.

You can plant hardy water lilies either when they are dormant or when they are actively growing. Plant dormant water lilies when the water temperature is 50° F. Most love locations with full sun, although a few do well in partly shaded spots.

'Marmorata', tropical, day bloomer

TROPICAL WATER LILIES

Water lilies from tropical climates are the most enchanting of all water garden plants. Their flowers exude an almost intoxicating fragrance. It is no surprise that they are often used in creating perfumes.

Tropical water lilies flower much more than hardy water lilies. The most common color is blue, but they also come in a range of lavender and purple, as well as pink, yellow, and white. Some are small and are suitable for container water gardens. Others can grow more than 8 feet in diameter in a single season, and one leaf alone may measure over 2 feet wide. The foliage is often mottled in purple or brown.

Some tropical water lilies are night bloomers, opening after the sun sets and staying open until late the next morning. These night-blooming lilies are especially suitable for gardeners who work during the day and come home after four in the afternoon, when the hardy water lilies have already closed. The night bloomers often flower in red, with rose, pink, or white cultivars also available. Red night bloomers may have maroon foliage. Tropical water lilies should be planted when the water temperature reaches 70° F, most in locations with full sun. A few will tolerate part shade.

TROPICAL WATER LILIES

- ◼ Sun (a few cultivars bloom even in part shade)
- ◼ Hardy in Zones 10 and 11 but grow anywhere having several weeks of 80° F temperatures
- ◼ Spread: varies with cultivar
- ◼ Height: floating, with flowers up to 12 inches above the water surface
- ◼ Water depth: 6 to 24 inches; some varieties tolerate deeper water, up to 6 feet
- ◼ Flowers: all summer in water over 72° F

'Colorado,' is hardy to Zone 5 with protection.

WILL IT FIT?

Water lilies are often referred to as being suitable for small, medium, or large ponds. Here are the general guidelines for the different sizes of water gardens discussed in this book.

Container garden	1 to 3 feet wide
Small pond	3 to 6 feet wide
Medium pond	6 to 10 feet wide
Large pond	More than 10 feet wide

Natural, or earth-bottom, ponds may be of any width but are usually at least 3 feet deep.

LOTUSES

Lotuses should be contained in the largest pot possible, or planted in contained bogs; they run freely by underground tubers that can otherwise overtake a pond.

LOTUSES

- Sun (a few cultivars bloom even in part shade)
- Hardy in Zones 4 to 11
- Height: miniature, 6 to 10 inches; dwarf, 10 to 12 inches; medium, 2 to 4 feet; larger, over 4 feet
- Spread: running; keep potted for best results
- Water depth: moist to 12 inches; some larger varieties tolerate water to 3 feet deep
- Flowers: 6 to 8 weeks beginning May or June in the Deep South, July farther north. Lotuses require several weeks of 80° F weather to bloom. In the South, plants may bloom a second time in September.

L otuses are among the most ancient of plants. Viable lotus seeds have been found dating back more than 2,000 years. Within the lotus genus *Nelumbo*, there are two species. *N. lutea* is the American native lotus, with creamy yellow flowers that are usually single, occasionally semidouble. *N. nucifera*, Asian lotus, usually has white or pink single, semidouble, or very double blossoms.

Although few improved varieties of the American native lotus have been selected, one U.S. hybridizer, Perry D. Slocum, has crossed *N. lutea* with *N. nucifera* to make free-flowering hybrids in new, rich colors. Slocum's additional contribution has been the introduction of lotus with blossoms that consistently rise above the foliage—an important trait because many forms have flowers that appear among or remain hidden underneath their large, parasol leaves.

Much hybridization has been done with the Asian lotus. Because of its exquisite flowers and unusual foliage, these lotuses have been grown and cultivated for hundreds of years, especially in China; at last count in China alone, over 600 varieties are recorded.

Gardeners around the world have profited greatly from these efforts. Lotus cultivars are available in a wide range of sizes and colors. Some selections are truly miniature, growing no more than a foot or so in height with flowers no larger than a tennis ball. Others are huge and stately, reaching over 6 feet tall, with leaves over 2 feet in diameter and flowers as large as basketballs. Fragrance varies from heady and fruity to mild, like baby powder. Colors range from the deepest rosy pink (there is no true red) to the cleanest white. There are also bicolors and tones that blush or fade.

Bowl lotuses from China are also available. Also called teacup lotuses, they are like standard lotuses in all respects except their size. They grow to no more than 2 feet in height, some only to 4 inches tall—perfect for tabletop ponds. Some cultivars grow much larger when planted in large pots, although they never reach giant size. Some of these change flower size and shape (by adding petals).

When growing bowl lotuses, be especially careful with the amount of fertilizer added during the growing season. Miniature lotuses burn more easily than standard-size plants. They are also more sensitive to pH, so make sure to use distilled water.

Lotus blossoms close very early the first day that they flower, often before dawn.

Hard tap water can burn the leaves easily. Rainwater may be suitable, depending on its acidity.

Lotuses are generally sun-loving plants that require at least 6 hours of sunlight each day. Only a few cultivars, such as 'Angel Wings' and 'Perry's Super Star', will grow and flower in part shade. Lotuses are not a tropical plant; they simply love hot weather, preferring warm soil and water temperatures. They revel in humid weather, and generally will not start to grow in spring until the pond water reaches 60° F. Consistent water temperatures are the best; temperatures that swing up and down will delay flowering and in extreme instances may send the plants into early dormancy. They flower several weeks later than water lilies, often not until July and August in Zone 5. In areas where the days are warm but the nights are cool, lotus grown in a freestanding pot can be covered with a plastic canopy to retain warmth overnight.

Lotus flowers open at different times during the day and night, depending upon the age of the blossom. First-day flowers usually open at about four or five in the morning, stay open for just three or four hours, then close around 8 a.m. On the second day, flowers begin to open just after midnight, at about 1 a.m. By seven or eight in the morning, flowers will be fully open. Again they stay open for only a few hours, closing around noon that same day. On the third day, flowers open in the dark,

around 1 a.m. They open fully by 9 a.m. By noon, they close but maybe not completely. On the fourth and final day, flowers open during the morning or afternoon. They will be faded and tattered and begin to shed their petals.

Lotuses are hardy water plants that overwinter even in cold climates. Cut back the foliage to the water surface after the leaves have died and turned brown. If you cut it while it is still green, fungal or bacterial infections can reach the underground tuber and kill the plant.

Care for lotuses as you would hardy water lilies, keeping the tubers deep enough in the pond that ice and frost will not reach them. In a shallow pond, this can be easier with lotuses than it is with hardy water lilies; lotus roots grow at the bottom of the pot, while lily rhizomes are often at the soil surface. In spring, bring the pot up to the surface, where the water and the soil will be warmed by the sun. If the lotuses are not overwintered in the pond, put the pot in a trash bag and store it where it will stay cool (but not freezing), dark, and damp.

Lotus blossoms are so large and their fragrance so heady that people sometimes liken them to flowering brandy snifters.

AMAZING ANCIENT LOTUS

In the years after World War II, a Japanese gentleman by the name of Dr. Ichiro Ohga attempted in vain to grow ancient lotus seeds excavated from a site near the Namegawa River in Japan. After his first attempts failed, he recalled that ancient lotus seeds had also been discovered at a site near the Kemigawa River. In March 1951, Ohga traveled to the area and enlisted help from local residents to find the lotus seeds. The volunteer crew, aided by children from the local elementary and high schools, dug for almost a month. At last they found the seeds, estimated to be more than 2,000 years old. Ohga set the seeds in water. Amazingly, they sprouted and grew. The resulting lotus now bears Ohga's name. A full-size lotus, 'Ohga' has stunning, dark pink, single flowers that look almost red when they first bloom. 'Ohga' is what lotus must have looked like centuries ago, when they were prized and revered in the Orient.

ARRANGING THE LOVELY LOTUS

The flowers, seedpods, and foliage of lotus look striking in floral arrangements. Lotus have been used for centuries in Buddhist ceremonies. In Indonesia, buds are stripped of their outermost sepals and placed among folded lotus foliage; they resemble delicate pink rosebuds. Flowers that have already opened are also highly decorative, with their outermost petals folded to look like pink ribbons. Blossoms are also attractive floating in a bowl of water, their powerful fragrance quickly filling the room. The foliage adds a dramatic flair to any arrangement; the seed heads last for years and work in both fresh and dried arrangements.

MARGINALS

ACORUS
Sweet Flag

Acorus calamus 'Variegatus' (above) grows to 3 feet tall. Japanese sweet flag has a similar, shorter cultivar.

- Sun to shade
- Zones 4 to 11
- 8 to 36 inches tall
- Running: to 18 inches wide, depending on cultivar
- Moist soil to 2- to 6-inch-deep water

Sweet flags are invaluable for their neat, clean appearance. Hardy and foolproof, they add textural interest to a pond. They need constantly moist soil; under-watering burns leaf tips. Most tolerate seasonal flooding; once mature, they can handle several inches of water over the crown. However, Japanese sweet flag can't take water over its crown for more than a few days.

All sweet flags can overwinter in the pond or in a mulched perennial border, but don't let them dry out. Propagate by dividing the rootstock, anytime from spring through fall.

Smaller forms are prone to spider mites. Larger selections may develop a fungus that causes black spots and can kill the foliage. Clean up dead foliage in fall; remove affected leaves if spots appear.

Sweet flag (A. calamus), green and variegated forms, are tall and upright. They grow from roots that run freely and form small clumps. Graceful 'Ogon' Japanese sweet flag (A. gramineus) has light green foliage with bright yellow stripes and is generally evergreen.

ALISMA PLANTAGO-AQUATICA
Water Plantain

The large leaves of water plantain stand erect above water. Flowers appear in late summer to fall.

- Sun to part shade
- Zones 3 to 11
- 12 to 36 inches tall by 18 inches wide
- Moist soil to 3-inch-deep water

Water plantain is an herbaceous perennial with spoon- or lance-shaped, deeply veined foliage. The leaves stand erect above the water when growing along the pond edge. Submerged leaves become long and ribbonlike. Blooms are larger at the bottom and taper to a point at the top. The flower, with large, pyramid-shaped heads, forms whorling white or pink clouds, appearing in summer and fall and lasting into winter.

Plants are suitable for medium to large ponds. If they are not dead-headed regularly, they self-seed and become invasive in an earth-bottom pond. During a dry season, seeds are prone to sprout to the point of being a nuisance along a shoreline.

Overwinter water plantain in the pond. Winter chilling is essential to its growth and flowering in subsequent seasons. Bulblike corms form at the base of the plant, and the leaves and roots die off completely in winter. Don't overlook them and toss them out during spring cleaning. You can propagate the plant in spring by growing seeds in wet soil or by dividing the corms.

ALTERNANTHERA PHILOXEROIDES
Alligator Weed

Equally happy in or out of the water, alligator weed blooms in summer.

- Sun to part shade
- Zones 9 to 11
- 2 to 6 inches tall
- Floating runners
- Moist soil to 3-inch-deep water

Alligator weed is a low-growing, tropical plant that provides cover and shade for fish. It trails on the water surface and will grow in hanging baskets. In water gardens, it clambers at the base of taller marginals, such as canna or umbrella grass.

Alligator weed grows equally well in or out of the water, but when submerged, it needs crystal clear water or it may rot. It is susceptible to spider mites and aphids.

Plants do not survive below-freezing weather, and overwinter best above 50° F. Grow them from seed or propagate them from stem cuttings, which quickly root in water.

Alligator weed leaves are small, rounded, and fleshy, held on large stems. Small, white, powder-puff flowers nestle near the leaf base. This species can be a nuisance in warm climates.

Copperleaf (A. reineckii), a related plant, has purple-red foliage accented by white summer flowers. It has an open habit that works in any size pond. It is best grown as a marginal; although it will tolerate deep water, it has a tendency to let go of the soil and root at the water surface.

BACOPA

Water Hyssop

- Sun to shade
- Zones 6 to 11
- 2 to 4 inches tall
- Creeping
- Moist soil to 6-inch-deep water

These dainty, low-growing tropicals make excellent ground covers in bog gardens and near the edge of ponds, and trail nicely in a waterfall or a tabletop pond.

Foliage is usually small, rounded, and fleshy. Tiny flowers bloom in summer and range from white to blue, depending on the species.

Leaves are often lemony fragrant when crushed.

Water hyssop grows year-round in warm climates. In cold areas, cut about 3 inches from several tips of the plant and place them in a cup of water in a warm, sunny room. They will root and grow during the winter. Replant them in a pot outdoors when all chances for freezing weather are past.

Water hyssop (*B. monnieri*), also called water purslane, has tiny, light green leaves and white summer flowers with faint pink stripes that look like ridges in the petal. It grows well submerged in clear water, but it does not produce flowers below the water surface.

Lemon bacopa (*B. caroliniana*) has large blue flowers as does variegated lemon bacopa (*B. lenagera*).

The pink stripes on the white blossoms of water hyssop are almost too faint to see.

CALTHA

Marsh Marigold

- Sun to part shade
- Zones 4 to 7
- 12 to 18 inches tall by 12 to 18 inches wide
- Moist soil to 1-inch-deep water

Favored by water gardeners because their bright yellow flowers open in early spring, marsh marigold has giant, lima-bean shaped leaves that are dark green, glossy, and toothed. Blooms are usually single but sometimes double. Plants grow in mounded clumps in moist to wet boggy conditions. In cool climates

they grow from spring through fall. In warm areas they may die back in summer.

Overwinter marsh marigolds in cool conditions so they bloom well the following season. Propagate by dividing offsets in early spring or by seed, although seed requires cold, moist stratification before sowing on moist spring soil, and seeded offspring may not grow true to form.

Marsh marigold (*C. palustris*), also called cowslip, is the most widely grown of all the species. The plant has been used medicinally but is poisonous if eaten raw. *C. palustris palustris* (syn. *C. polypetala*) is more hardy and vigorous, and its flowers may be twice the size. It grows

18 to 24 inches tall with a 12- to 24-inch spread.

Marsh marigolds start spring off right. They are among the earliest blooming plants in a water garden.

CANNA

Water Canna

- Sun to part shade
- Zones 9 to 11
- Height varies with cultivar
- 2 to 3 feet wide
- Moist soil to 10- to 12-inch-deep water

True water cannas (*C. glauca* and *C. flaccida*) grow well in saturated soil with water over their crown. They have attractive foliage and yellow blossoms. Other cannas, such as the common garden canna (*C. × generalis*) are terrestrial but adapt to waterlogged soil.

Tall and impressive and growing several feet tall in a single season, cannas are topped by colorful flowers that start in midsummer and last until frost. Canna foliage is large, long, and tapered, ranging from bright green to blue-green, dark purple or crimson, to striped in yellow, white, or red. Flowers also come in a wide variety of colors, from delicate creams and yellows to brassy oranges and reds with either large, overlapping petals or a more delicate, narrow form.

Cannas cannot withstand a freeze. Bring them indoors for the winter; let the rhizomes dry out, then clean and store them. Propagate cannas by division.

Aphids and Japanese beetles affect plants in summer, spider mites in winter. Canna rust may occur if the plants dry out or the tubers are not cleaned well before storage.

'Erebus' is a Longwood hybrid aquatic canna.

CAREX

Sedge

- Sun to shade
- Zones 4 to 11
- 6 to 12 inches tall by 6 to 12 inches wide
- Moist soil to 1-inch-deep water

The V- or M-shaped leaves give sedges a grassy appearance. This is 'Oheme' palm sedge.

Sedges are grasslike plants whose mounded tufts of foliage will ornament the pond, water garden, stream, or waterfall—even a container planting. Several species are truly aquatic, and many prefer moist soil. Stems are triangular; leaves are V- or M-shaped, with a distinctive midrib rising from the clump and often arching up and out. Flowers are unremarkable—brown spikes that on certain species you'll find only with some investigation.

Sedge meadows along the shores of lakes or ponds are an important part of wetland ecology. They fill in gradually as the shoreline recedes, replacing plants that grew when the waters were deeper. Most sedges may be propagated from seed or from division of the rhizomes in early spring.

Bottlebrush sedge (*C. comosa*) is distinguished by long, brown, double-toothed spikes emanating from the sheathlike structure around the seed. The effect is striking, reminding one of a long, fluffy cluster of grass. Leaves are M-shaped and rough along the margins. It grows to 2 feet high with a 2½-foot spread in moist soil to 3-inch-deep water.

Blue sedge (*C. flacca*) is a worthy addition to the shade garden, although it also grows well in full sun. It makes a perfect companion to hostas in the damp, shaded bog garden. The cultivar 'Bias', a variegated blue sedge, adds a cool blue and white margin and lights up the darkest corner of the bog garden or the pond.

Inflated tassel sedge (*C. fascicularis*) has large, puffy seed heads that resemble spiny cucumbers; they are attractive in dried arrangements The plant grows to 2 feet.

Palm sedge (*C. muskingumensis*) is often used to reclaim wetlands. It is easy to grow and forms a clump much like a hosta. It tolerates full shade yet also grows in full sun, where it will take on a golden green cast.

COLOCASIA ESCULENTA

Taro

Taro evokes a tropical mood in any garden. Black-leaved forms like this 'Jet Black Wonder' also add color.

- Sun to part shade
- Zones 9 to 11
- 2 to 6 feet tall by 2 to 4 feet wide
- Moist soil to 6-inch-deep water

Bold and large-leaved, taro (also called elephant's ear) thrives on fertilizer and hot, humid weather. Ideal for container gardens as well as full-size ponds because of its eye-catching foliage and graceful habit, it produces larger leaves if it is protected from the afternoon sun. The petiole, or leaf stalk, comes in many beautiful colors, so locate the plant to show them off.

Overwinter plants indoors by keeping the pot in a saucer of water in a warm, sunny room. Or you can let the plant dry out, then dig the corms and store them in coarse vermiculite in a sealed container or in a cool (but frost-free), dark spot. The corms will remain dormant until brought out again in spring.

Propagate from corms that are divided from the main plant, or from "hulis" (top or side sprouts).

Transplanting every year will keep plants healthy. Older plants tend to grow smaller tops and are more prone to rot.

'Black Magic' taro has very dark, almost black-purple, leaves and stems. 'Metallica', violet-stemmed taro, is particularly elegant, with deep purple stems and large, velvety, blue-green leaves. 'Chicago Harlequin', discovered at the Brookfield Zoo in Chicago, Illinois, has stems that are striped in purple and white, with large leaves that are finely marked and veined in purple.

Black princess taro (*C. jensii*) is slightly shorter than some of the others and has bright green leaves and stems with blue-purple blushing between the veining. The plant has a clumping habit.

Another, related genus is *Xanthosoma*, which includes tannia. A favorite tannia is *X. sagittifolia* 'Chartreuse Giant'. Growing to 2 or 3 feet in height, it has very large, elephant-ear-shaped leaves that are a bright lemon gold. It lights up even the shadiest pond.

CYPERUS

Cyperus

- Sun to part shade
- Zones 7 to 11
- 2 to 12 feet tall by 2 to 5 feet wide
- Water depth: Varies with species

Related to the sedge family, cyperuses are tropical water plants grown for their sprays of ornamental leaf fronds, which resemble small paper umbrellas. The large heads are held high atop triangular stems sprouting from a central clump. "Flowers" are small and green and turn tawny brown as the seeds develop. There's a species of cyperus—from very large to very small—for every pond. Some have open, grassy heads with thin, wiry leaves. Others are dense, bushy, and full. Cyperuses shade shorter plants at the edge of the pond. Besides having ornamental value, they are excellent filtrators.

All species are heavy feeders, and you should fertilize them at least once a month. Only a few species are hardy in cold regions, but plants overwinter easily in a greenhouse. Although you may grow cyperus from division, umbrella grass is often propagated by cutting off the fronds just below the point where they join the stem. Trim the foliage to an inch and float the head in water. When it sprouts new stems and grows roots, you can plant it in a pot with soil. Cyperus also grows easily from seed, sown on moist soil and kept warm until they sprout.

Umbrella grass (*C. alternifolius*) is the most commonly sold species. Its top leaf sprout can grow up to 2 feet in diameter in mature specimens and form the characteristic umbrella shape for which the plant is named. Individual leaves are about half an inch wide and a foot or more in length. A quick grower, umbrella grass usually requires division every few years to keep the center from becoming woody and empty of foliage. New stems will grow from the outer edge of the base, creating a ring around the corky middle of the plant. Dwarf umbrella grass (*C. alternifolius* 'Nanus') is a compact plant that has long, umbrella fronds. It's hardy in Zones 9 to 11 and grows to 2 feet tall. It tolerates moist soil and up to 4 inches of water over its crown.

Papyrus (*C. papyrus*) and Mexican papyrus (*C. giganteus*) are favorites of many water gardeners. Papyrus is stunning, with its 10-inch ball of long green threads; Mexican papyrus has 20-inch spheres of wiry foliage on stiff, erect, nonarching stems. Both are hardy in Zones 8 to 11 and grow in moist soil to 12-inch-deep water. They grow 5 to 12 feet tall and spread 4 to 5 feet.

Dwarf umbrella grass displays small, green-turning-tawny-brown flowers in summer.

Dwarf papyrus (C. isocladus) grows to 18 inches tall and is hardy to Zone 9.

Papyrus has much finer texture than many of the other cyperuses.

DICHROMENA COLORATA

White-Top Sedge

- Sun to part shade
- Zones 8 to 11
- 1 to 2 feet tall
- Running
- Moist soil to 1-inch-deep water

The seed bracts of white-top sedge resemble 3-inch stars floating above grassy foliage. The flowers are actually small, fuzzy things clustered in the center of white bracts. After a time, both the flowers and the surrounding spikes turn light brown, retaining their starlike appearance. They make excellent cut flowers and dry well.

White-top sedge has a running habit and is best confined to a pot. Division after a few years is recommended; the plant grows in a circle around the outer edge and in a few years the center of the pot will have few sprouts of new foliage. It requires no other special care or maintenance but appreciates monthly doses of fertilizer.

D. colorata is closely related to *D. latifolia*, and the two are often sold interchangeably at nurseries and garden centers. The white seed heads of *D. latifolia* are about one-third larger than those of *D. colorata*. Plants overwinter well in a sunny greenhouse or in the house. Propagate them by dividing the rhizomes.

The star-shaped flowers (inset) of white-top sedge float above the plants. The petals are actually bracts.

EQUISETUM FLUVIATILE

Water Horsetail

Horsetails offer a stiff upright form rare among water plants. A dwarf species is available.

- Sun to shade
- Zones 4 to 11
- 2 feet tall
- Running
- Moist soil to floating

Water horsetail has green stalks with large, black bands accented by thin pink bands. It branches freely and grows very thin, long side shoots that radiate from each main stem. There are roughly 30 species of *Equisetum* but only a few are truly aquatic, although several adapt well to wet soils. They are easily identified by their straight, hollow stems, which are grooved. Each joint is a distinct part of the stem and has a black band at its edge.

Plants reproduce by spores borne on cones that grow atop each stem and so are classified as cryptogams, plants that bear no flowers or seeds.

Equisetum earned the common name horsetail because the stems resemble the tail of a horse. The plants' uptake of silica, which is deposited as silica crystals in the tissue, causes their stems to be hard and gritty. Because of this, they were much favored to scrub pots and pans and earned the name scouring rush from early pioneers.

Extremely cold-tolerant, horsetails survive winter at the pond edge. They are usually propagated by dividing their underground rhizomes in spring.

GLYCERIA MAXIMA VAR. VARIEGATA

Variegated Manna Grass

Like many ornamental grasses, variegated manna grass spreads freely and needs restraint.

- Sun to part shade
- Zones 4 to 11
- 1 foot tall
- Creeping
- Moist soil to 3-inch-deep water

Variegated manna grass is a rambling aquatic with 2-inch-wide leaves that are usually a foot or so in height. Its foliage is striped in creamy white and bright green. In spring and fall, when the weather is cool, the leaves take on a delightful pink tinge. The plant spreads freely and should be restrained in a pot. In earthen plantings, it should be placed next to a mowed edge, which will keep it in check.

Manna grass generally overwinters easily in the pond. It requires submersion under only enough water to cover the crown of the plant, with no need to move it deeper into the pond. Plants grow by underground rhizomes that are easily divided in spring.

Although the species is an important food source for wildlife, the plant is not ornamental, and for this reason only the variegated cultivar is commonly available at nurseries or garden centers.

Water hibiscus is a true aquatic, tolerating 2-feet-deep water during seasonal floods.

HIBISCUS

Hibiscus

- Sun to part shade
- Zones 5 to 11
- 4 to 6 feet tall, 2 to 4 feet wide
- Moist soil to 6-inch-deep water

Hibiscus are large, coarse-textured perennials that resemble shrubs. Flowers are brightly colored and often as large as a dinner plate.

Water hibiscus (*H. moscheutos palustris*) is a true aquatic, thriving in wet soil to flowing water. It branches freely and has pink flowers with a rose throat. It tolerates seasonal flooding, up to 2 feet deep.

Swamp mallow (*H. moscheutos*) has stunning, 10- to 12-inch flowers in colors ranging from white through deep red. It is usually larger-flowering and bushier than water hibiscus but not as water-tolerant. It will tolerate seasonal flooding.

It dies back to the crown in winter and may be slow to appear in spring. The plant attracts butterflies and hummingbirds. New cultivars with stunning, summer-long blooms include 'Copper King' (red cut-leaf foliage and red or pink 12-inch-wide blooms) and 'Blue Danube' (large, pristine white flowers). *H. militaris* also tolerates wet soil. It is hardy to Zone 6 and warmer regions.

HOUTTUYNIA CORDATA 'CHAMELEON'

Houttuynia

- Sun to shade
- Zones 5 to 11
- 6 to 8 inches tall
- Running
- Moist soil to 1-inch-deep water

This lizard's tail relative is a rampant runner in moist soil with the potential to become invasive. Confine its roots in a pot or with some other barrier.

Plants have heart-shaped leaves that form a dense mat and have a spicy fragrance when crushed. In fall, they turn dark maroon-purple. 'Variegata' is similar but has green and white leaves without red or maroon.

White, single-petaled flowers appear in late summer. The green form of houttuynia flowers freely, starting in summer and continuing through early fall. Double-flowering 'Flora Pleno' houttuynia has small, white blooms that resemble rosebuds.

Houttuynias are excellent ground covers. Try them under the upright stalks of iris or butterfly plant (*Asclepias incarnata*). They grow well in a bog or other wet spot. Don't let plants freeze; submerge them in the pond.

Versatile 'Chameleon' houttuynia grows in sun or shade, soil or water. Blooms have less punch than foliage.

HYDROCOTYLE

Pennywort

- Sun to part shade
- Zones 7 to 11
- 1 to 4 inches tall
- Running
- Moist soil to 4-inch-deep water

Pennyworts are low-growing aquatics with round, often toothed leaves that are fleshy and shiny and stand up straight from running stems. They may be a ½ inch to 3 inches in diameter. Plants quickly shade the pond as they grow running stems that float out over the water surface, scrambling between plants and making a soft edge between water and taller plants. In a container, they spill over and trail downward from the pot edge. They are usually grown for their foliage; flowers are inconspicuous white tufts that often remain underneath the round, umbrella-like leaves.

For tender species grown in cold climates, bring the stem cuttings indoors. They will root in warm water on a sunny windowsill. Cold-tolerant species overwinter well at the bottom of the pond with water lilies.

Hairy pennywort (*H. americana*) is one of few pennyworts with noticeable white flowers, which rise above ½-inch to 1¾-inch foliage in white tufts. It trails freely and is an excellent plant for waterfalls or pond edges or in a tub garden or tabletop pond.

'Little Umbrellas' pennywort is aptly named, although other pennyworts have similar, nasturtium-like leaves.

HYGROPHILA

Hygrophila

- Sun to shade
- Zones 9 to 11
- 1 to 3 feet tall, 1 to 2 feet wide
- Moist soil to submerged

Most hygrophila have tiny snapdragon-like, blue flowers. Their leaves are usually long and narrow, becoming wider toward the middle. Some plants have ruffled leaves. Many species are sold as aquarium plants, some of which are also suitable as marginal plants.

Dragon lantern (*H. stricta*) is an upright fast-grower with purple-tinted foliage in cool spring and fall weather. It is free-flowering and tiny blue flowers often cover plants near the main stem year-round.

Water wisteria (*H. difformis*) has mintlike foliage and tiny blue flowers that hang from trailing stems. Plants will grow submerged in water, in which case their foliage becomes finely cut and fernlike. 'Variegata' has strong white leaf veins. Both the green and variegated selections are excellent plants for containers or small ponds, trailing over the edge of the pot and filling in empty spots between taller, more upright plants.

Propagate plants by stem cuttings, which will root in warm water.

Dragon lanterns bloom in summer. Cool weather brings out a purple tint in the foliage.

IRIS

Iris

Tall-statured yellow flag has the typical flower of an iris. It grows just as well in gardens as beside ponds.

- Sun to part shade
- Zones 4 to 9
- 2 to 4 feet by 1 to 2½ feet wide, depending on species
- Moist soil to 3- to 6-inch-deep water

Two types of iris grow in and near the pond. True water irises include yellow flag (*I. pseudacorus*), blue flag (*I. virginica*), southern blue flag (*I. versicolor*), and rabbit-ear iris (*I. laevigata*). These species grow best with water over their crown throughout the year, even in fall and winter. Others, such as Japanese iris (*I. ensata*), tolerate wet soil for part of the growing season, but they prefer drier conditions.

All irises bloom in spring in colors ranging from white to deep blue with purple and lavender hues. Some are deeply veined or marked with yellow toward the center of the petals. The flowers generally rise above the leaves of the plant, often appearing to float on water.

Water garden irises need minimal attention through the summer but are subject to a few maladies, such as thrips and root knot. Plant and transplant them immediately after they have finished flowering, but mulch them heavily later in the summer to withstand the winter cold. Propagate iris by division or from seed after six weeks of cold, moist dormancy.

Yellow flag iris owes its name to its bright yellow, early-spring flowers. Both blue flag and southern blue flag have light blue flowers in midspring, and their blue-green, sword-shaped leaves take on a dark red stain from the base to the tips.

Rabbit-ear iris has rounded, short, upright petals in white, elegant blue, or royal reddish-purple blooms. In cool summers, it usually reaches only 12 to 18 inches tall.

Japanese iris has flowers 6 inches or more in diameter held above the foliage. They may be single, double, or multiple-petaled. Colors range from deep, velvety purple to the cleanest white. Generally, blooms are flat and petals hang downward.

JUNCUS

Rushes

- Sun to part shade
- Zones 4 to 9
- 2 to 3 feet tall by 2 feet across
- Moist soil to 4-inch-deep water

'Gold Strike' (left) and 'Spiralis' (right) demonstrate the variety found among the several species of rushes.

Many rushes have strong, upright foliage, which provides a useful background for other pond-side plants with either a bolder or more delicate nature. Most rushes are noted for their long, spiked stems, which are usually dark green but can be light blue. Foliage is stiff and hollow. Flowers appear as brown tassels that droop from near or at the tip of the leaves.

In many climates rushes are evergreen. They should occasionally be cut back to the ground to remove older, tattered growth. Plants may be grown in the perennial border as long as they are given adequate moisture.

Stands of rush are useful in earth-bottom ponds, providing spawning ground for bluegills and sunnies. Dragonfly larvae often use the upright leaves to rise from the water, clinging to the foliage while they metamorphose into adult dragonflies. The plants provide important shelter for fish, fowl, and insects.

Most rushes are cold-tolerant and may be overwintered in the pond. Bring tender species such as Australian silver rush (*J. polyanthemos*) indoors, treating them like houseplants.

Rushes grow from underground rhizomes that are linked by stolons and are easily divided.

Soft rush (*J. effusus*) has stiff spines of green foliage. It often retains its color all year, even in cold climates. Corkscrew rush (*J. effusus* 'Spiralis') has tightly coiled foliage, which is excellent in fresh or dried floral arrangements. It is almost evergreen even in cold climates. 'Gold Strike' has dark green leaves accented with gold stripes along their length. Both plants are hardy to Zone 3.

Blue rush (*J. inflexas*) has baby blue foliage, which resembles that of blue fescue. It grows in full sun and takes moist soil to 2-inch-deep water. It is hardy to Zone 4.

JUSTICIA AMERICANA

Water Willow

- Sun to part shade
- Zones 4 to 11
- 1½ feet tall by 1 foot wide
- Moist soil to 10-inch-deep water

A hardy relative to the shrimp plant, water willow produces masses of 1-inch clusters of white to pink flowers. The foliage is narrow, like willow leaves. Plants are shrubby.

Water willow grows about 18 inches tall in moist soil or in several inches of water. It also tolerates running water. It is extremely useful in earth-bottom ponds and is an excellent plant for erosion control. Inexplicably, water willow is underused in water gardens or in reclamation projects.

Divide water willow rhizomes in early spring before new growth appears. Plants are also easy to propagate from stem cuttings.

For large ponds, water willow creates a fishable edge that holds the soil, yet is so open that fishing lures will not snag or become hung up in it. Planted at the edge of the pond, it also somewhat deters geese, keeping them from wading into the water. Because water willow tolerates some disturbance and trimming, it can be grown around boat docks and landings.

Water willows have white to pink blooms in summer on a versatile, easy-to-grow plant.

LOBELIA

Lobelia

- Sun to part shade
- Zones 5 to 11
- 6 to 60 inches tall, depending on species
- 12 inches wide
- Moist soil

A favorite for the bog and perennial garden, lobelias are cherished for their brilliant flowers, which appear in late summer through fall. Their flowers, which have divided petals with two tips pointing upward and three downward, somewhat like a split-petaled snapdragon, attract butterflies and hummingbirds. Flower colors vary from bright red or bright blue through crimson and purple. Some have purple or dark red foliage. Plants do not usually branch; each stem grows from a separate crown.

Two of the most common lobelias are cardinal flower (*L. cardinalis*) and great blue lobelia (*L. siphilitica*). Cardinal flower has bright, crimson-red flowers July through September on 3-foot-tall stems. Great blue lobelia is similar to cardinal flower in form and habit, with bright blue blossoms July through October.

It is best to place plants deep in the pond for the winter or mulch them in a perennial bed. Lobelia is easily propagated by division in spring. Cardinal flower and great blue lobelia may also be propagated by floating mature stems in water; plantlets sprout at leaf nodes.

Late-blooming cardinal flower adds a bright splash of color to moist sites near ponds or in gardens.

LUDWIGIA

Ludwigia

- Sun to part shade
- Zones 6 to 11, depending on species
- 6 to 96 inches tall, depending on species
- Trailing to 24 inches wide
- Moist soil to floating

Ludwigias range in size from huge (over 8 feet tall) to tiny (less than 6 inches tall). Leaves are usually rounded, toothed, and shiny. Flowers are mostly yellow, single, flat, and four-petaled. Often, they form pneumatophores—spongy white spikes at the base of the stem that help plants absorb oxygen from water. Frost-tender species are best overwintered as houseplants in cold climates or as stem cuttings grown on a warm, sunny windowsill in a vase of water.

Primrose creeper (*L. arcuata*) is a good pond cover, creating an unusual visual effect in the water garden. As it floats out over the water, it holds the last 6 inches of its foliage straight up from the water surface. Flowers are bright yellow and about an inch wide.

Red ludwigia (*L. repens*), a creeping form, has bright green leaves on red stems. This small plant is ideal for a waterfall or as ground cover at the edge of a pond or bog. It is hardy in Zones 5 to 11 and grows 6 to 10 inches high.

Primrose creeper is a short ludwigia that spreads to 2 feet wide. Its yellow flowers appear in summer.

Water Clover

- Sun to shade
- Zones 5 to 11, depending on species
- ¼ inch to 6 inches tall, depending on species
- Running
- Moist soil to 4-inch-deep water

Mimicking a four-leaf clover, floating water clover is actually a fern. It grows to 6 inches tall with an indefinite spread.

The distinct notch in the leaflets helps separate cutleaf water clover from other species.

Hairy water clover has a no-frills, modern appearance.

Water clovers are the lucky charms of the pond. Their four-leaf, clover-shaped foliage belies the fact that they are really ferns, which reproduce by spores.

The plants are easy to grow and not particularly heavy feeders, so fertilize sparingly. They prefer shallow water that is rather still, and they are perfect for small ponds. Water clovers are not difficult to overwinter in cold climates, provided they do not freeze solid. Place them toward the bottom of the pond with other frost-intolerant aquatics, such as hardy water lilies and lotus.

Most species have foliage that emerges above the water surface; the leaves of one species float on the water. The emerged leaves open in the morning; when they close at night, they look like small butterflies at rest. All species have four lobes to each leaf. Some species have hairy leaves, others smooth.

In very cold climates, overwinter water clovers by bringing plants indoors and keeping them as houseplants. They are easily propagated by stem cuttings.

Floating water clover (M. mutica) has shiny, waxy-looking leaves that grow from small, clublike, spore-bearing structures. Not a heavy feeder, it does best in still water and is grown easily from root cuttings. Plant it when the water temperature reaches 60° to 65° F. When crowded, it will send up leaves that stand 3 inches out of the water. Until then, the leaves float on the surface. In cold climates, bring it indoors and keep it in a bowl of water near a warm, sunny window. The cultivar 'Micro Mini' has dense

The 1-inch-wide leaflets of butterfly water clover have wavy edges. Leaves open and close daily.

leaves about the size of a dime that float on the water surface or rise slightly above the water. It is ideal for container water gardens.

Hairy water clover (M. drummondii) has silvery, clover-like foliage that is accented by brown stems. The leaves look like resting butterflies. It grows to 6 inches tall in moist soil to 1-inch-deep water.

Upright water clover (M. quadrifolia) has very upright, triangular leaves. It is good to grow near waterfalls and for giving small fish a place to hide. It is a rampant grower, hardy to Zone 5.

Butterfly water clover (M. rotundifolia) is covered in 1-inch leaves that open and close daily. Hardy to Zone 8, it grows to 6 inches tall in moist soil to 6-inch-deep water.

Cutleaf water clover (M. schelpeana), with its irregularly cut foliage, has a lacy, delicate air. Hardy to Zone 6, it grows to 6 inches tall in moist soil to 3-inch-deep water.

MENTHA

Water Mints

- Sun to part shade
- Zones 5 to 11
- 3 to 12 inches tall
- Running
- Moist soil to 2-inch-deep water

Many mint species are highly fragrant and have long been used for their aromatic qualities. Several species are tolerant of wet soils, even those usually grown in the perennial border, such as spearmint. Mint has attractive, evenly green, lance-shaped leaves, which are often hairy, especially on the bottom. Flowers are clustered balls of tiny blue or pink flowers, appearing in midsummer and continuing through fall. Because of their running habit, mints should be kept in containers. They tolerate freezing temperatures and require no special care in cold climates. Water mint is easy to propagate, especially from stem cuttings or by division.

Aquatic mint (M. *aquatica*) is always a favorite with water gardeners. It is highly fragrant, flowers well, and attracts butterflies. The foliage is scented and can be used in teas and jellies.

Brook mint (M. *pulegium*), a ½-inch-tall version of aquatic mint, has airy, dainty flowers of sky blue.

It is just as fragrant as other mints and attracts butterflies. It's perfect for growing among rocks or in the nooks of a bog garden.

Water mints contribute fragrance to water gardens, and, like other mints, they can be used for cooking.

MIMULUS

Monkey Flower

- Part to full shade
- Zones 5 to 11
- 12 to 36 inches tall by 12 to 20 inches wide, depending on species
- Moist soil to 6-inch-deep water

Monkey flowers are best known for their tubular flowers, which resemble open snapdragons. They range in color from blue to lavender or purple, or occasionally white and yellow. Although they grow adequately in full sun, they prefer part shade, where they grow taller and stay greener. Deadheading encourages more blooms and stretches the growing season. Plants winter well in cold climates. Propagate by division or seed.

Sharp-winged monkey flower (M. *alatus*) has stalked leaves and winged stems. Flowers are usually lavender, but there is a rare white-flowering form, 'Snow Crystal'.

Lavender monkey flower (M. *ringens*) has profuse lavender flowers peeking out from between shiny, jade green leaves that are oblong, unstalked, and toothed.

Yellow monkey flower (M. *guttatus*), with yellow blooms, is not as cold-tolerant as other monkey flowers species.

Red monkey flower (M. 'Lothian Fire') has bold, bright red trumpets with yellow throats. Plants are well accented by shiny green foliage on red stems.

Like all mimulus, lavender monkey flower has two-lipped blossoms in summer. Plants prefer shade.

MYOSOTIS SCORPIOIDES

Forget-me-not

- Sun to part shade
- Zones 5 to 9
- 6 to 8 inches tall by 12 inches wide
- Best in running water, such as streams

This front-of-the-pond marginal rings in early summer with sprays of white, light blue, or bright blue flowers resembling small, single roses. Plants have small, somewhat hairy, oblong, clear green leaves. They form a dense mat that also grows well in a stream or waterfall.

Forget-me-nots often flower intermittently throughout the summer as long as it's cool. In warm, humid climates, plants wither and leaves may turn dark. Trim wilted leaves; the plants will perk up when cooler days return. In southern climates, forget-me-nots are best grown as a winter annual.

It is difficult to distinguish the forget-me-nots that grow in water gardens from those that prefer dry land. If it grows in the pond, it is the aquatic form; if it withers and starts to die in the pond, it belongs in the perennial bed.

'Mermaid' has large blue flowers dotted with white eyes. 'Pinkie' forms a creeping cushion of cotton-candy-pink flowers. The crystal white flowers of 'Snowflakes' open in spring and continue through summer with larger and longer-lasting blooms.

Forget-me-nots, with their small blue blossoms, prefer cool climes. Flowers have white, pink, or yellow eyes.

MYRIOPHYLLUM AQUATICUM

Parrot's Feather

Looking very similar to foxtail, parrot's feather grows only 6 inches tall and has denser foliage.

- Sun to part shade
- Zones 6 to 11
- 6 inches tall
- Running
- Moist soil to floating

Parrot's feather has whorls of feathery foliage, which floats out over the water surface at the edge of the pond. Whorls may be 3 inches or more in diameter, growing on long, trailing stems. Although some references list this species as a submerged, oxygenating plant, foxtails (M. *heterophyllum* and M. *hippuroides*) and several other species are the ones that grow underwater (see page 23).

Because parrot's feather grows rampantly, it has earned a place on the prohibited noxious weed list in some states. Before buying plants, check with authorities to ensure that it is allowed in your state, especially if you live in a warm climate. In climates where frost occurs, there is less chance of it escaping from your water garden and becoming a nuisance.

The plant may survive a winter freeze if submerged beneath the water, but it is not reliably hardy in cold areas. To ensure survival, overwinter parrot's feather by bringing stem cuttings indoors.

OENANTHE

Water Parsley

'Flamingo' water parsley is nearly as colorful as houttuynia, but it grows much taller.

- Sun to part or full shade, depending on species
- Zones 5 to 11
- 6 to 12 inches tall, depending on species
- Spread varies
- Water depth varies

Water parsley has finely cut foliage resembling leaves of celery or parsley. Leaves are aromatic and edible, having a peppery flavor suitable for salads and stuffings. Foliage grows from running stems that root quickly at the leaf nodes. Flowers are umbels of small, white, starlike blossoms appearing summer through fall. The plants are excellent for filtration, taking up nutrients that would otherwise contribute to algae. Water parsley winters easily in cold climates and withstands freezing.

Rainbow water parsley (O. *javanica* 'Flamingo') has pink, white, and green frilly foliage that resembles compact carrot tops. It grows well along the edge of the pond, stream, or waterfall or in a large container water garden. This cultivar exhibits a running spread and grows in moist soil or floats.

Common water parsley (O. *sarmentosa*), with its lush green foliage, provides an excellent foil to larger, more full-leaved plants. It grows rapidly and can cover a small pond in a single summer.

PHYLA LANCEOLATA

Frog Fruit

Tiny frog fruit blossoms, also called fog fruit, start out white, as here, then change to yellow, then pink.

- Sun to part shade
- Zones 5 to 11
- 2 inches tall
- Trailing
- Moist soil to 4-inch-deep water

An ideal ground cover for a wet spot in the yard or for a rocky margin at the edge of the pond, frog fruit tolerates some foot traffic and may even be mowed. It has small, lance-shaped leaves that are toothed and an even green color. In fall, foliage turns a wonderful crimson. Starting in early summer and lasting through fall, the plant is covered in tiny white flowers that resemble those of verbena. As the flowers mature, they change to yellow, then pink.

Plants overwinter well in northern climates without special care or attention. Leave them in the pond or at the water's edge. Propagate plants from stem cuttings.

Frog fruit adapts well to many situations and conditions. In a container or tabletop pond, it will spill over the edge or tuck itself between more upright stems of other marginals. In a bog, it's an excellent ground cover. It even grows in the moist shade between pavers. In an earthen pond, frog fruit helps to control soil erosion around docks and boat landings. Regardless of its environment, it always attracts butterflies and skippers, who relish its sweet nectar throughout the summer.

PONTEDERIA CORDATA

Pickerel Weed

- Sun to part shade
- Zones 5 to 11
- 24 to 30 inches tall by 12 to 18 inches wide
- Moist soil to 10-inch-deep water

Pickerel weed, also called pickerel plant and pickerel rush, is favored for its shiny, heart-shaped leaves and striking blue or white flowers in summer. It has a compact habit and a rhizome that grows like an iris near the soil surface.

It is also appreciated for its excellent filtration abilities. The cultivar 'Crown Point' has been rated as one of the best overall filtration plants in studies performed by Dr. Michael Kane at the University of Florida in Gainesville.

The winter tolerance of pickerel weed depends heavily on its local heritage. Buy plants that have been grown for the particular climate in which you will raise them.

Flowering habits also vary. When the flowers have finished, the spikes often lean into the water to disperse seeds downstream. The flowers attract butterflies, skippers, and hummingbirds. Dragonflies and damselflies use the upright stems as perches to shed their final larval stage before becoming adults.

Seeds and leaves are edible. Young leaves can be used in salads or cooked as vegetables. Seeds may be eaten like nuts or ground to make a flour.

The species has shiny, jade-green, heart-shaped foliage and large blue flower spikes. 'Alba', white pickerel weed, has flowers that are white rather than blue and tinged in pink, especially at the base. Leaves are shiny, green, and rounded. 'Pink Pons', lavender pickerel weed, has lavender-pink flowers.

'Crown Point' is more compact and bushy than the standard pickerel weed; its leaves and flower spikes are more rounded as well; and it is extremely hardy. It grows to 1½ feet tall in moist soil to 6-inch-deep water. Hardy in Zones 4 to 11, 'Crown Point' is well-suited for northern wetland sites, especially with its ability to filter pollutants from the water.

'Spoon River' has narrow, ¾-inch-wide spoon-shaped leaves to 7 inches long. Flowers are intensely blue and stay erect after blooming.

The southern counterpart to 'Spoon River' is *Pontederia cordata lancifolia*. It, too, has narrow, more elongated foliage and bright blue flowers. For flowers during the shorter days of winter, gardeners grow 'Singapore Pink', a tropical form of pickerel plant. It has light pink flowers from October until April. It is best grown indoors as a houseplant in winter, brought

outdoors to the backyard pond when the water warms.

Plants overwinter best in cold climates if rootstocks are protected from freezing. Place rootstocks well below the frost line of the pond or remove plants and store them in cold, damp quarters until spring. Propagate pickerel weed by dividing rootstocks in spring. It may also be grown from seed but requires a period of cold, wet dormancy.

'Crown Point' pickerel weed grows to about half the size of standard pickerel weeds. It is also hardier than the species.

RUELLIA BRITTONIANA

Water Bluebell

- Sun to part shade
- Zones 9 to 11
- 2 to 4 feet tall by 1 foot wide
- Moist soil to 6-inch-deep water

Ruellia that grow in wet soil are often sought by water gardeners. They are most noted for their large, petunia-like flowers that appear all year long in the tropical climates they prefer.

In cold climates, the foliage often turns dark purple when night temperatures cool. Because plants do not withstand cold temperatures, they must be wintered indoors as

houseplants. Propagate them from stem cuttings and from seed.

The species is a favorite; it is easy to grow and is covered with 1- to 2-inch, lavender-blue flowers. 'Chi Chi' is a delightful pink variation with foliage that turns burgundy in fall. 'Katie' is a dwarf water bluebell with blue flowers that nestle tightly against the stems. It is compact, usually reaching no more than 10 inches or so in height, but its flowers are the same size as those of the standard water bluebell. 'Strawberries and Cream' is a new cultivar with variegated leaves speckled in cream, pink, white, and green. Flowers are soft purplish blue. Plants grow to 10 inches tall.

Water bluebell blossoms range from white to pink to blue.

'Katie' is a new dwarf cultivar. Look for named selections to ensure uniform flower color and plant size.

SAGITTARIA

Arrowhead

Arrowheads earn their name from their distinct leaf shapes. Expect plants to bloom in summer.

- Sun to part shade
- Zones 3 to 11
- 3 to 10 inches tall
- Running
- Moist soil to 2-inch-deep water

Arrowheads contribute to the water garden landscape with its clean, geometric foliage and delicate white flowers. Named for its arrow-shaped leaves, arrowheads are highly ornamental at the pond edge and very easy to grow.

Foliage may be broad or narrow, depending upon the species; some have lobed leaves. Flowers are single, white, and held on a long stalk that rises from the center of the plant, appearing first in June and recurring through the summer.

Ruby-eye arrowhead, or giant arrowhead (*S. montevidensis*), has red dots at the base of each petal. It is 2 feet tall (Zone 8). Common arrowhead (*S. sagittifolia*) grows to 18 inches (Zone 3). Lance-leaved arrowhead (*S. lancifolia*) has yellow-centered blooms and grows to 2 feet (Zone 8). Red-stemmed arrowhead (*S. l. ruminoides*) has burgundy-red stems. 'Crushed Ice' (*S. graminea*) has white-variegated leaves. It does best with afternoon shade and is 1 foot (Zone 5). Another cultivar, 'Bloom'n Baby', is a dwarf, free-flowering arrowhead that starts to bloom when the plant is only 3 inches tall.

SAURURUS

Lizard's Tail

The goose-neck blooms of common lizard's tail last all summer. A red-stemmed variety exists.

- Sun to part shade
- Zones 4 to 11
- 1 to 3 feet tall
- Running
- Moist soil to 6-inch-deep water

Lizard's tail species are known for their heart-shaped leaves that appear on tall stems growing from creeping rhizomes. The plant forms dense colonies of upright stems topped with drooping spikes of white flowers. Both the flowers and the stems are aromatic, with a fragrance similar to vanilla.

Although lizard's tails will withstand a frost, they cannot tolerate being frozen in the pond. They must be placed so that their underground rhizomes won't freeze during winter. They grow well from stem cuttings or rootstock divisions.

Common lizard's tail (*S. cernuus*) is well-suited to the water garden, providing a tall backdrop for smaller plants. Its white flowers last from June through frost and return year after year. There's also a variety with red stems, *S. cernuus ruminoides*.

Chinese lizard's tail (*S. chinensis*) has a white splotch on the topmost leaf, making the plant ornamental even when it is not in flower.

SCIRPUS

Rush

Growing with a grassy habit, rushes have brown, not particularly ornamental, flowers in summer.

- Sun to part shade
- Zones 3 to 9
- 4 to 6 feet tall
- Running
- Moist soil to 6-inch-deep water

Rushes are excellent for shoreline stabilization in a natural pond or stream. They provide important cover for wildlife, such as birds and amphibians, as well as nesting grounds for wildlife and fish.

Foliage is thin, narrow, and tall; flowers are brown clubs or plumes that appear in mid- to late summer. Many species are cold-tolerant and will survive a winter freeze. Most commonly propagated by division, rushes may be grown from seed.

Woolly rush (*S. cyperinus*) is distinguished by its fluffy, silken tassels of tawny brown at the end of stiff, dark green foliage. The plant forms a dense clump and does not run, unlike other species.

Giant nut grass (*S. fluviatilis*) boasts tall parasols of emerald green foliage. It grows 2 to 4 feet tall and does best in full sun.

Zebra rush (*S. zebrinus* syn. *Schoenoplectus lacustris tabermaemontani* 'Zebrinus'), is ornamental from spring through fall with white bands or markings every few inches along its tall green leaves. The white bands are more pronounced in cool weather or when the plant is actively growing.

STACHYS PALUSTRIS

Marsh Betony

- Sun to shade
- Zones 4 to 8
- 6 to 24 inches tall
- Running
- Moist soil to 5-inch-deep water

Prized by herbalists in the middle ages, marsh betony is now finding popularity among water gardeners. You may be familiar with this plant's close relative, lamb's ears. Marsh betony is much different. It has thick spikes of pink or purple flowers resembling those of snapdragons or penstemons. Plants bloom throughout the summer into fall and are a welcome substitute for purple loosestrife (*Lythrum* spp.), a noxious, prohibited weed that chokes out wetlands.

Marsh betony has hairy, lance-shaped leaves with serrated edges. Bright green in summer, the foliage turns bright yellow in fall, adding interest to the pond even after flowers have faded.

Propagation is easy. Divide the clump in early spring when it first starts to sprout. Plants can also be propagated by stem cuttings, which root easily. Perfectly winter-hardy, marsh betony requires no special care or treatment to survive freezing weather.

Related to mints, marsh betony has dark green foliage and two-lipped pink flowers in midsummer.

THALIA

Thalia

- Sun to part shade
- Zones 5 to 11
- 2 to 9 feet tall by 3 feet wide
- Moist soil to 12-inch-deep water

Thalia (also called alligator flag) is grown primarily for its striking, lush foliage. Leaves can reach 3 feet wide and over 3 feet long. Flowers are unusual, silvery purple beads that droop from long, arching stems.

Purple thalia (*T. dealbata*) overwinters in cold climates without protection. Alligator flag (*T. geniculata*) is more tender and will not survive frost. Bring it indoors for the winter. Thalias are propagated most readily by rootstock division.

'Blue Cup Leaf Form' purple thalia has blue leaves that are more cup-shaped than others. 'Broad Leafed Form' has flat leaves that are triangular. The foliage looks tropical and has a slight powdery blue color.

Alligator flag derives its name from the fact that the plant sways like a flag in the presence of alligators. As the gator swims through the glade, it rustles the plant, causing the leaves to swing back and forth. Foliage is more yellow-green than the hardy forms of thalia, and the plants grow 2 to 9 feet tall.

The flowers of purple thalia rise high above the leaves on long stalks. Plants bloom in late summer.

TYPHA

Cattail

- Sun to part shade
- Zones 3 to 11
- Height varies
- Running
- Moist soil to 4-inch-deep water

Cattails grow in freshwater marshes and colonize wide areas with their stiff, running rhizomes. They thrive in water over their crown and provide habitat for fish and amphibians. Their foliage serves as a nesting source for many species of wild birds, and their roots are often eaten by muskrats.

The leaves of cattails are $\frac{1}{16}$ inch to 2 inches wide. They are generally flat on one side and more rounded on the other. Flowers are long catkins that turn brown as they mature, releasing downy seeds. There are also giant and dwarf forms; plant height can range from 6 inches to over 12 feet tall.

Plants overwinter well in cool water and withstand freezing temperatures. They propagate quickly from division of rhizomes and can be grown from seed.

Common cattail (*T. latifolia*) is the standard cattail seen in ditches and wetlands. It is excellent for water filtration. Graceful cattail (*T. angustifolia*) is narrow-leaved, with foliage that arches and sways gracefully. Very elegant, it's suitable for most ponds and large container water gardens.

Graceful cattail has finer-textured leaves and smaller catkins than common cattails.

SOIL, FERTILIZER, AND WATER

Many products are available to fertilize water garden plants. Use the liquid form in bogs and containers where you won't have to worry about causing an algae bloom. Tablet-form fertilizers can be used just about anywhere.

Water gardening begins with plants. Pot them up, then put the pots in the pond. Make sure that you fertilize correctly, the plant is at the right depth, and good, clean water is in the pond, and you're on your way to being an ace water gardener. There's no trying to figure out if you've over-watered or under-watered, if the soil is too dry or too moist, or if you've waited long enough to water again.

SOIL

The first step to growing water plants is planting medium. The best one for all water garden plants except filtrators is clay soil. That may come as a surprise to perennial gardeners because clay, with its dense, water-retentive nature, is the worst soil for perennials. These same qualities, however, make it ideal for water plants.

Clay stays soft in water, which allows roots to penetrate it. It is composed of small particles, which hold fertilizer like a sponge until the plant needs it, reducing the amount of fertilizer

that leaches into the water. Sandy or loamy soil or even silt will work if they are at least half clay (or if you can add that much clay). You can tell if your soil is clay by making a small ball in the palm of your hand. Push your finger into it; if it doesn't break up, it's clay.

If you don't have clay soil or you're in doubt about the composition of your soil, add clay to the mix. Or add generic, nondeodorized, nonscoopable kitty litter. It's nothing more than clay from decomposed limestone—perfect for most water plants. Also, it doesn't float once it's wet and won't dirty the pond the way soil does if spilled. Either mix kitty litter half and half with soil or use it alone in pots.

Some commercial water garden potting soils are available from manufacturers such as Fafard and Scotts. These are heavy, unamended soils made specifically for water plants. Avoid potting mixes and other commercial soils for perennials or annuals, especially the lightweight mixes with peat moss, bark, perlite, vermiculite, and other lightweight ingredients. In water, these float out of the pot and create a mess on the water surface. Also, as the organic matter decomposes in warm water, it releases harmful amounts of organic salts and removes most of the oxygen in the root zone, killing roots.

Filtrating plants have different soil needs. Their roots take in unwanted nutrients in a pond with fish and so must be exposed to water. Alternative planting mediums for them include pea gravel, cocoa fiber, rock wool, synthetic fiber, baked-clay-based soil (Profile), and clay-sand-and-decayed-granite mixes. These allow roots of filtrators in open-weave pots to grow beyond the pot. Although you can use these materials with other water plants, they're not the best choice. Stick with clay, kitty litter, or commercial water gardening soils.

FERTILIZER

Water plants, like all plants, need nutrients. To ensure that they get what they need, fertilize them. The best kind of fertilizer is one designed specifically for water plants. These can be in liquid, granular, or tablet form.

Liquid fertilizers are good for container water gardens or plants you can take out

Clay

Kitty litter

Pea gravel

Commercial soil

Profile

of the pond and fertilize in a bucket of water. Don't pour liquid fertilizer into a pond. Algae will absorb most of the nutrients.

Use granular fertilizer to mix into potting soil when planting or dividing plants. Tablet (or tab) forms look like large pills. To use them, simply poke them into the potting soil.

Avoid "once-a-season," timed-release products. These work by osmosis or by having a coating that slowly dissolves. In a water garden, where the fertilizer is in constant contact with water, the pellets dissolve rapidly, adding too many nutrients to the pond at once. Also avoid using tree spikes and organic fertilizers. In water, tree spikes release their nutrients right away, burning the roots around them. Plus, they leave behind hard spikes, which can accumulate. Cow, sheep, and pig manure, bat guano, and kelp extract are fine in cool water, but in warm water, they quickly foul a pond or rot roots.

Whatever you use, know how long it takes to dissolve so you will not add it too often. Drop a sample in a bucket before mixing it with the potting soil. Note how long it takes to dissolve completely. Most tablet forms should last two to three weeks underwater. Granular products last about six weeks.

WATER

Although you can't overwater plants in a water garden, you can underwater them. Each type of plant has its own tolerance for fluctuations. For this reason, keep your pond within 1 to 2 inches of its designed depth at all times.

Falling water levels expose the liner, which looks tacky. Worse, if you use a pot without a hole and the water level drops below the top of the pot, the plant can dry out in a day or two. Top off the pond, letting water trickle out of the hose on the pond bottom so that it doesn't dramatically change water temperature. Only add up to 10 percent new water at a time. On very hot days, oxygen levels drop. Splatter the water into the pond to mix air into it.

WATER QUALITY WITHOUT FISH: Except for floaters, pond plants tolerate water in a wide pH range—5.5 to 9.1—and aren't affected by the chemicals used to treat municipal water. However, they don't tolerate salt from excess fertilizer or water softeners. Planting directly into a clay-bottom pond buffers the water from wide pH swings. Even so, don't fill the pond with water recycled from a water softener.

WATER QUALITY WITH FISH: If the pond contains fish, water quality is a major concern. Before stocking the pond, treat the water with dechlorinator and chloramine remover to eliminate chlorine, chloramines, and heavy metals.

MYTH OF THE BALANCED POND

Sometimes water gardeners are led to believe that their pond will reach a "natural equilibrium" if they follow a mathematical formula of plants and fish—a state at which everything is in balance so the pond never needs cleaning or fertilizing. Not true. Ponds are dynamic artificial environments. All parts of a pond contribute to overall health and well-being. Ponds change daily, and while ratios and rules of thumb are helpful guides learned from experience, they don't eliminate all the work. Our role is to direct the parts—and take satisfaction in doing so.

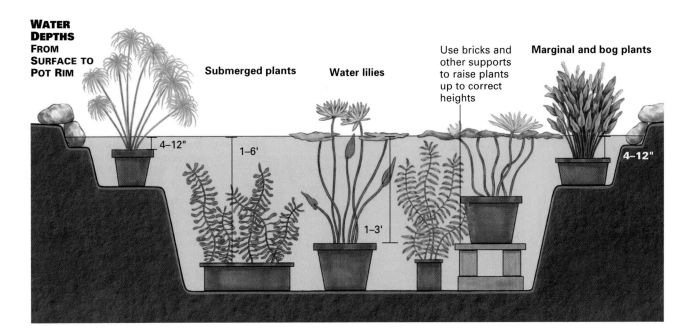

WATER DEPTHS FROM SURFACE TO POT RIM

Submerged plants

Water lilies

Use bricks and other supports to raise plants up to correct heights

Marginal and bog plants

4–12"

1–6'

1–3'

4–12"

POTTING UP

Standard pots as well as newer designs can all be used to hold water plants.

The purpose of a pot is to keep plant and soil together in the pond where you want them to be, without dirtying the water or damaging the pond. Many types of pots are available, and most serve their function well. It's important to know the relative benefits and drawbacks of each type, so you can choose the one that's right for the way you want to grow the plants in your pond.

MESH CONTAINERS: Open-weave or plastic-mesh pots and fabric baskets are favored for filtrators because they allow roots to grow through them and have more contact with the water. These are the containers you often find for sale in the water garden section of a nursery.

Transplanting from an open-weave pot may be more difficult because, as plants mature, their roots naturally grow thicker and may become entwined in the plastic. If you wait too long to divide and transplant nonfiltrating plants with running stems, such as lizard's tail, cattail, and rushes, their roots may grow together between pots, making them doubly difficult to remove from the pond. Such root growth is also a treat for large, hungry fish, so if you don't want your plants to become a salad bar for koi, and you want trouble-free transplanting, transplant as soon as you see the roots growing into the water.

TRADITIONAL POTS: Nursery containers and clay and plastic pots with single or multiple holes make good homes for most water garden plants, including water lilies and water-lily-like plants—even plants that run. Single-hole nursery pots are especially good for containing running marginals such as phragmites and lizard's tail. The single hole prevents—or at least slows—plant roots from growing out of the pot. Containers without drainage holes, especially decorative pots, are excellent for miniature ponds on a tabletop or patio.

Because traditional pots let water in from the bottom, they also keep plants from drying out if the water level drops below the lip of the pot. If you use a container that has no holes in a large pond, however, take care that the lip of the container is always below the water surface so that the plant doesn't dry out.

SIZE: Pot size should be matched to the size and type of plant. Because most water plants grow only in the top 10 to 12 inches of soil, that's as deep as the container needs to be. Any deeper, and the soil generally is wasted. Some plants don't need this much soil, growing only an inch or so deep. A few, such as lotuses and 'Victoria' water lilies, however, need a much deeper pot. In fact, lotuses will send roots down as far as 3 feet. For help in

GAUGING THE POT SIZE

Plant Type	Best Pot Size
Marginal	1 gallon
Water lilies	17 inch
Lotus	23 inch
Water-lily-like	1 gallon
Submerged, creeping	Cat litter tray
Submerged, noncreeping	1 gallon

selecting the right-size pot for your plants, see Gauging the Pot Size on page 48.

POTTING UP

When you get ready to pot up water plants, prepare a spot where you can set up everything you'll need. First, choose a shaded area in which to work. Direct sunlight beating down can be extremely damaging to water plants as you wash soil off their roots and transplant them. This location should be close to the pond, so you can easily get the plants back in the water. If there's no shade near your water garden, fill a wading pool with water and hold the plants in it until you're ready to restock the pond.

Next, gather your supplies. You'll need soil, pea gravel, pruners, and running water from a hose.

To pot water plants, the basic steps are to trim off any dead or damaged plant parts, then partly fill the pot with soil, set the plant in the pot, and finish filling the pot, avoiding covering the crown. Leave enough room to add a layer of pea gravel on top. Where these steps differ is in how deep you set plants, where in the pot you set them, and how much fertilizer you mix in. You can mix fertilizer into the soil before filling pots, using amounts recommended on the label, or use tablets, as shown in the illustrations on this and the next two pages.

POTTING UP WATER LILIES

Water lilies are easy to plant when they're small. The method you use depends upon whether they are hardy or tropical lilies. Hardy water lilies can be planted dormant, when they have few or no leaves, or when they are in active growth, with leaves and roots that have already sprouted. Tropicals are generally shipped—and planted—in full,

active growth, when they don't have a tuber. Although you can plant them while they still have tubers, it's more difficult.

HARDY WATER LILIES: To plant a dormant or actively growing hardy water lily, fill your pot about two-thirds full of soil. Make a mound in the middle of the pot with a handful of soil. Place the rhizome on the mound, then spread any roots over the top of the soil so they are not under the rhizome. Sprinkle soil over the roots and around the rhizome, adding just enough to cover the rhizome. Do not bury it. It should have no soil on its crown; otherwise, it will have difficulty sprouting new leaves. Water the pot thoroughly, then top it off with pea gravel, again avoiding covering the crown.

**TROPICAL
WATER LILY**

TROPICAL WATER LILIES: Tropical water lilies require a little detective work to plant at the right depth. Examine the lily's stems, starting at the base. Look for the point where the stem changes color from light to dark. This is the point from which the leaf emerged from the soil. When you plant the lily, the topping-off material must be even with this point. This will ensure that you have the plant's growing crown (the union where the roots meet the stems) at the right depth.

It's important that the main growing crown of a tropical be planted at just the right depth. If it is planted too deeply—especially on a night-blooming cultivar—it will usually stop growing in order to make new plants, taking energy from the main crown. You will eventually have more new plants, but they will be smaller, and by the time they reach the size at which they will bloom well, it may be too late in the season for them to set flowers.

The general planting procedure is the same as for hardy water lilies. Fill the pot about two-thirds full of soil, form a mound in the middle of the pot, place the base of the plant over the mound, spread the roots out, and cover them with more soil. Leave enough room to top them off with pea gravel at the color change on the stem.

BOTH TYPES: Water lilies are extremely buoyant when in leaf. Even rhizomes of dormant hardy water lilies have been known to suddenly pop out of the pot and float to the water surface after transplanting. If you are planting the lilies when they are actively growing, try to retain as many roots as possible and anchor them by firming the soil

HARDY WATER LILY

POTTING UP
continued

around the roots. For large plants, place a smooth rock on top of the soil over the rhizome (of a hardy water lily) or over the roots (of a tropical water lily). Keeping the plants just 4 to 6 inches below the water surface until their roots have a firm grip on the soil—three to four days in warm water—also helps to reduce buoyancy.

MARGINAL WATER PLANTS

Marginals grow in a wide variety of ways. Some develop from underground rhizomes, others from a central crown, and still others crawl across the soil surface. Here are the basic categories of marginal plant growth habits and the ways in which the types are planted. For all plants bought at a nursery, find out what material they've been transported in. If it's organic matter, such as peat moss or bark, shake the plant free of the bulk of the organic matter and pot in kitty litter or heavy clay soil. Pot them up in at least a 1-gallon container. South of Zone 7, you'll need a 2-gallon container.

MARGINAL WITH RHIZOME

RHIZOMATOUS MARGINALS: Water iris, sweet flag, and other marginals grow from a rhizome. To pot them, first fill the pot with soil about one-half to just under two-thirds full. Place the rhizome slightly off-center, with its cut end toward the edge of the pot. For water iris, especially, this allows the fan to grow toward the center of the pot. Next, spread the roots over the soil, then fill the pot with more soil to just cover the rhizome. Top off with pea gravel. If the water temperature is over 60° F, poke a regular dose of fertilizer tablets into the soil.

SINGLE-STEMMED MARGINALS: Lizard's tail, houttuynia, water willow, golden candles (*Lysimachia punctata*), and other marginals form a colony of individual stems that grow in a clump. Because all of these plants root from their stems, they should be planted with their roots well below the soil surface. Fill the pot about two-thirds full. These plants are sold in bunches of individual stems, or you can use cuttings. Select five to 15 rooted stems (less than five looks skimpy), poke a hole in the soil in the center of the pot, and place the stems in the hole. Firm the soil around them, adding more to fill the pot but leaving room to top off the pot with gravel.

The potting technique for Japanese sweet flag falls somewhere between that of water iris and lizard's tail. The plant looks like an iris, which is planted on the edge, but it actually needs to be planted in the center, like a lizard's tail. Plant several fans per pot; one fan alone looks sparse. Fill the pot two-thirds full of soil, then set the rhizomes in the center of the pot with their fans facing outward in a roughly triangular fashion. This helps them to branch out and fill the pot, and to form a cluster in the center of the pot. Finish filling the pot, using enough soil to anchor the fans firmly in place, then top it off with gravel.

MARGINALS THAT GROW FROM A CENTRAL CLUSTER OF STEMS: Umbrella grass, sedges, and rushes send up clusters of stems from one central crown. Stems of umbrella grass and sedges generally sprout from the crown and grow in groups of three; rushes sprout any number of stems at the outside edge of the crown.

To pot these marginals, fill the container two-thirds full. Place the plant in the center, spreading the roots around the pot. Then cover the crown or rhizome with about an inch of soil to help anchor it. Top off the pot with pea gravel. Don't submerge the pot for the first week (at least); the stems are buoyant and may pop out. Instead, put the pot in water only as deep as the crown.

MARGINALS THAT GROW FROM A SINGLE CROWN OR TUBER: Similar to the group above, these plants have multiple stems anchored in a central crown or tuber. Pickerel weed, water plantain, lobelia, monkey flower, bog arum (*Peltandra virginica*), and golden club (*Orontium aquaticum*) are potted in much the same fashion as the other marginals discussed here. Fill the pot about two-thirds full of soil, place the plant in the center of the pot with its roots spread over the soil, then cover them. Make sure the crown of the plant is about an inch below the soil surface. Top off with pea gravel.

SINGLE CROWN OR TUBER

ARROWHEAD: When potting arrowhead that is actively growing, treat it as you would other plants that grow from a central crown. But when potting up dormant tubers, you need to use a different technique.

In fall, arrowhead forms a tuber. Technically a turion, it is the reason why arrowhead is often called duck potato. The turion resembles a small potato and is a favorite food of waterfowl. In spring, the turion sprouts and sends a runner to the soil surface. Once it reaches the surface, the runner sprouts a single plant with a central crown. If you are potting up turions, plant them well toward the bottom of the pot. Fill the pot one-fourth full with soil, set the tubers on the soil, then finish filling the pot. The turion will elongate and grow a new plantlet at the top of the soil.

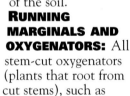

ARROWHEAD

RUNNING MARGINALS AND OXYGENATORS: All
stem-cut oxygenators (plants that root from cut stems), such as foxtail, anacharis, and fanwort, and running marginals, such as cattails, are planted in a similar way. First, fill the pot with soil and top it off with sand or pea gravel. Water the soil thoroughly so it is easy to work. Using your finger, poke a hole in the soil about 1½ to 2 inches deep. If the pot is small, make just one hole. If the pot is large, make several holes around the perimeter as well. Insert anywhere from five to 10 stems in each hole. Firm the soil around the stems and submerge the pot in the pond. You can also plant oxygenators by gently tying them to a rock and placing the rock on the bottom of the pond. For the plants to overwinter, though, press their stems into the soil so that the plants root.

WATER-LILY-LIKE PLANTS: Treat water-lily-like plants much like oxygenators. The rule of thumb is one plant in a 6-inch pot, three in a 10-inch pot, and three to five in a 12-inch container. Fill the pot with soil, top with sand or pea gravel, and water thoroughly. Then make a hole in the soil, place the crown of the plant about an inch below the soil surface, and firm the soil over the roots. Submerge the pot in the pond roughly 6 inches below the water surface. Because their stems are so brittle and dehydrate so easily, water-lily-like plants should be kept as moist as possible while you are working with them and be returned to the pond as soon as planting is done.

TOPPING OFF

The final step of potting all water plants is to top off the soil with pea gravel or one of the commercial baked-clay-soil products. When dry, these products are lighter than gravel and may be easier to use. Topping off helps keep the soil from being disturbed by circulating water and discourages nosy fish from rooting around and spilling soil into the pond. Pour a 1-inch-deep layer of the topping-off material over the soil, or add enough to fill the pot even with or slightly below its rim. If you have large koi in your pond, use large stones, such as smooth river rock, to cover the soil.

WATER DEPTH FOR PLANTS IN POND BOTTOM

Most water plants benefit from being planted directly in soil on the bottom of the pond, giving the roots unrestrained growth. This is best in a pond for wildlife and one needing only minimal cleaning.

PROPAGATING PLANTS

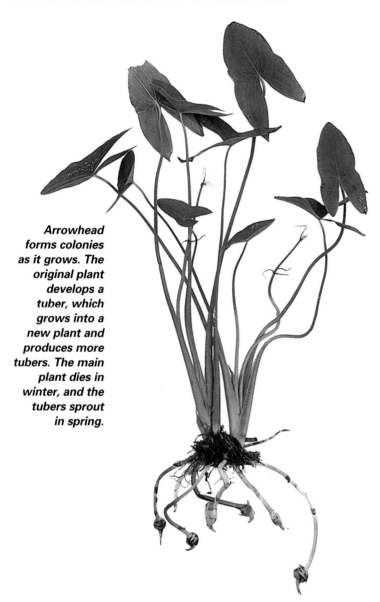

Arrowhead forms colonies as it grows. The original plant develops a tuber, which grows into a new plant and produces more tubers. The main plant dies in winter, and the tubers sprout in spring.

The easiest way to gain new water plants is to divide them. Just as when planting new water plants, choose a shady spot in which to work and have everything arranged for your propagating adventure. For container plants, your first step will generally be to remove the plant from the pot. To do this, gently roll the side of the pot on a hard surface and work the root ball out.

DIVIDING WATER LILIES

Water lilies are easy to divide. Do it in spring or early summer so the new plants have ample time to recover and harden off for winter. Wash soil from the rhizomes to find the small "eyes" that have sprouted here and there. Look for eyes that have a few leaves and

roots; cut the entire eye, along with the roots and leaves, from the main root with a sharp knife. Let leafless eyes continue growing for later divisions. Plant the new starts in fresh soil so that the leaf sprouts are just at the soil level.

In early summer, some water lilies produce young plants in the center of their leaves called viviparous growth. Some day-blooming tropical water lilies are especially prone to doing this, as are a few hardy water lilies from time to time, and some water-lily-like plants such as water snowflakes and water poppies. Pin the leaves with plantlets to the soil with a rock. Once the plantlets sprout roots, cut off the old leaf and plant the new water lilies in their own pots.

DIVIDING MARGINAL WATER PLANTS

As you might expect, the techniques for dividing marginals fall into the same categories as for potting up new plants.

RHIZOMATOUS MARGINALS: Divide these plants in summer after they flower. Break apart a large clump with a shovel or pitchfork, then replant each piece. For more precise division, wash the roots and look for the spot called the "fan," where the leaves emerge from the rhizome. If you want a good-sized plant in a 1-gallon pot, divide the rhizomes so that there are three fans to each pot.

SINGLE-STEMMED MARGINALS: Divide the clump of plants into four or five sections, slicing through the soil and roots as if you were cutting a thick pie into wedge-shaped pieces. Plant the sections as described on page 50.

Another propagation method is to take stem cuttings. Wash the roots and cut the rhizomes into 4-inch-long sections, each with a growing tip and a bit of runner. Plant them so the tips stand upright and the runners lie horizontally about an inch below the soil surface.

MARGINALS THAT GROW FROM A CENTRAL CLUSTER OF STEMS: Although all these plants are easily divided by splitting the crown with a sharp knife, members of the *Cyperus* family are also commonly propagated by soaking the "umbrella" cluster in a shallow bowl of water. New plantlets will sprout from the center and take root in just a few days to a week. Once they have grown a few inches tall, transplant them into a pot, where they will quickly mature.

MARGINALS THAT GROW FROM A SINGLE CROWN: The crown of a plant is the point at which the roots and stems meet. Propagate marginals that grow from a single crown by division in summer, which gives the new plants enough time to recover and harden off before winter.

First, wash the roots. Once the soil is gone, you will find new plants attached to the main, or mother, plant. Cut or split off any that have roots and leaves from the main plant and pot them up, making sure the crown of the new plant is about an inch below the soil surface.

ARROWHEAD: In summer, divide arrowhead in the same way as you divide plants that grow from a single crown. In spring, propagate them from the turion, as described on page 51.

RUNNING MARGINALS AND OXYGENATORS: Because these plants grow readily from stem cuttings, they are most commonly propagated by simply snapping off 4- to 6-inch-long pieces of the newest growth at the point at which it joins the main plant. Bind several stem cuttings together with a rubber band, fill a pot with moist soil, then make a hole and gently push the cuttings into the it. The stems will sprout new roots and overcome any transplant shock in just a few days.

WATER-LILY-LIKE PLANTS: These form individual plantlets right next to one another. To divide, simply remove each individual plant and pot it up as for other plants.

VIVIPAROUS MARGINALS: Some water plants, such as melon sword, sprout new plantlets along their growing stem or along flowering branches, similar to the houseplant spider plant. Separate this young growth from the main plant after it has sprouted a few roots. Or bend the branch so the plantlet is touching soil; pin it in place until roots have started to form.

Dividing iris: The plants form new fans with rhizomes that can be detached. First, identify the new fan and check it for roots. Then cut the new fan free from the original plant with at least 1 inch of rhizome and a few roots.

Cut the foliage on the new transplant to about 3 to 4 inches tall. Pot the rhizome and place it in the shade for a few days to give it a chance to recover.

For plants that grow easily from stem cuttings, propagation is a snap. Simply cut 4 to 6 inches of new growth from the plant. Remove the leaves at the cut end of the stem, about halfway to two-thirds up the stem. Place the stem cuttings in water until they root, or plant the stems directly in soil, so that the bare stems are covered and the leaves are above the soil line.

For running plants such as clover, take a 6- to 12-inch runner and cut it free from the main plant. Wind it in a circle around your fingers with the leaves to one side (up) and the roots to the other (down). Now place the circle on the soil, leaves up, and hold it in place with a bent paper clip.

POTTING AND DIVIDING LOTUSES

LOTUS RHIZOME

— Growing point or tip

Rooting—
at second
node

First node or joint

Lotuses are running plants that produce new rhizomes every fall. The rhizome is really a stem that grows horizontally in the mud. It consists of a growing point, followed by nodes or swollen lengths of stem, and joints. The rhizome usually consists of one to three of these joints. Small lotus varieties can be as short as 4 inches long, large varieties 2 feet or more.

Spring—before the tuber has had a chance to sprout and grow—is the best time of year to plant or divide lotuses.

Once the lotus has a few leaves, it's too brittle to survive being split apart and moved to new pots. Potting up or transplanting a lotus in spring is easy. You just have to know what you're looking for: bright, crisp, white rhizomes similar to elongated potatoes.

POTTING LOTUS

It's best to use a round pot when planting lotus. The rhizome will run in the pot and may break and die if it encounters a hard corner that it is unable to turn. Larger lotuses can be planted in pots that are 2 to 3 feet in diameter and a foot or more tall.

Lotuses grow better when there is 12 inches of soil in the pot, so use deep pots for these plants. Because this means that the pot will be heavy, some water gardeners prefer to keep their lotus in wheeled, decorative containers on their deck or patio. This is easier than trying to move the pots around in the pond.

It's not a good idea to grow lotus directly in the soil of an earth-bottom pond because they run and can take over the garden in a couple of years. It's better to plant the tubers in a large container and sink it into the pond. Once a lotus has had one flower, it will produce one flower bud at every leaf axil— the point where the leaf joins the stem—that follows. In a pond, the leaf axils are often several feet apart. This means that the flowers will be several feet apart, too.

STARTING LOTUS

There is an old, reliable Chinese method of starting lotus from bare-root rhizomes. The Chinese float them rather than planting them. Fill the pot in which you'll grow the lotus—one with no holes—almost full with soil, leaving room at the top of the pot for standing water. Pour enough distilled water into the pot so there's at least 2 inches of water over the soil. Drop the rhizome in the water; it will float.

It's best to use distilled water, as opposed to tap water or well water; distilled water is neutral—neither acidic nor alkaline— and sterile. Other kinds of water may contain contaminants or be too hard. Hard water contains many minerals, which raise pH, and high pH inhibits lotus growth. Move the pot to a spot where you can keep the rhizome warm (around 70° F) and it has lots of sun.

Once it has sprouted a few leaves, gently push the rhizome down so that it just touches the soil. Hold it in place with a flat stone. Don't try to bury the rhizome; it will grow roots and pull itself down into the soil. With this technique, you can count on a 99 percent success rate in starting your lotus. Even if the growing tip has broken—which generally means the rhizome won't sprout—this method works.

After the lotus sprouts, you can add it to the pond. Prop it up on bricks to bring it close to the water surface.

FERTILIZING

Lotuses are heavy feeders. Fertilize them regularly throughout summer, especially when they are in flower. But wait to fertilize until the tuber has sprouted at least three leaves. If you fertilize too soon, you can burn the plant.

When you do fertilize, follow the directions provided by the fertilizer manufacturer. You can use any material, as discussed on pages 46 and 47. If you use tablets, push them as far as possible into the soil, so the fertilizer reaches the lotus rhizomes at the bottom of the pot. Firm the soil over the fertilizer tab, so the fertilizer doesn't dissolve into the water and feed the algae in the pond.

DIVIDING LOTUS

Lotuses are usually divided in early spring before they have started to actively grow. First, gently turn the lotus pot upside down on an even, flat surface. You want the soil from the bottom of the pot—where the lotus rhizomes grow—facing up.

Very gently, wash away the soil with a stream of water from the hose until all of the rhizomes are free. As you free them, you'll find joints where sections meet, and growing points at the end, or tip, of each rhizome.

Starting at the tip, work your way back along the rhizome toward the center. Count back two joints, then cut into the next or third section with scissors or a sharp knife. Dividing the rhizome in this way protects the cutting if the sliced end rots. The joint prevents infection from spreading to either of the sections or the growing tip. Take special care not to break off the growing point; the plant may not sprout without it. Once you've made your divisions, follow the directions for potting bare-root lotus.

Your divisions should have at least one growing point, but often you'll have more. The more growing tips per division, the fuller the plant will be.

Turn the plant out of the pot, then gently hose it off to reveal the white rhizome, which grows on the bottom of the pot.

Lotuses grow well in their own bog garden. Simply scoop out a hole about 3 to 4 feet across and 2 feet deep. Line the hole with flexible liner and place a short piece of drain tile on end in the hole. Fill the hole around the tile with clay soil to a few inches short of the surrounding soil level. Plant the lotus tuber so that it's just below the soil surface and fill the hole with water. The lotus will root and soon fill the bog. In cold climates, lotus overwinters with little or no protection; its tuber migrates deeply into the soil to avoid freezing.

Find the end of the rhizome, using the photo on page 54 as your guide. Count back two sections and cut 1 to 4 inches behind the second node, or joint. You may find several sections to plant.

Fill a no-hole container to within 2 inches of the top with soil. Lay the tuber on top of the soil and fill the pot with water if putting it in a pond. Place a rock on the tuber between the nodes to hold it down. Don't bury it.

PESTS AND DISEASES

Water garden plants are generally fuss-free, only occasionally falling prey to insects or disease. Animals may visit the pond, damaging plants when foraging for food or using the habitat. Here are the more common problems that can plague plants in and around a water garden.

Dragonflies eat up to 200 mosquitoes a day; the immatures eat mosquito larvae in the pond.

CHINA MARK MOTHS

The most well-known pond insect pest is probably the China mark moth. Adult moths lay eggs on the leaves of water lilies, and the larvae drill into the central leaf stem, where they feed and grow for several weeks. The larvae may also chew small half-moon shapes from the outer edge of the lily leaf, using the cutout to make small enclosures on top of or on the underside of the leaf.

If only a few China mark moth larvae have attacked your lilies, remove and destroy them by hand. If the infestation is large, chemical treatment may prove effective. A dusting of *Bacillus thuringiensis* (Bt) will reduce and eventually destroy a population of China mark moth larvae without harming fish.

to use on or near ponds. You can remove either the fish or the plants from the pond before beginning treatment, but check the label to ensure that you can return them to the pond after treatment.

APHIDS

Most plentiful in late summer when the weather is hot and humid and rainfall scarce, tiny insects called aphids attack new leaves and young flower buds as well as aging, yellowed foliage. They especially go after water lilies and marginals. Aphids draw fluids and sugars from the plant, and in small numbers they are more unsightly than harmful. Left alone, their numbers can grow rapidly and soon harm the plant's growth and overall health.

The easiest treatment is to submerge the plant entirely below the water surface for a day or so. The aphids cannot survive underwater and will float to the top, where you can skim them off. A dusting of diatomaceous earth will also kill the aphids, although it may have to be repeated over several days in order to be effective.

JAPANESE BEETLES

Japanese beetles seem to prefer the leaves of thalia, curling the edges and creating an open-weave pattern in the foliage. They also damage cannas, especially those with red or orange flowers. If only a few beetles are affecting your plants, remove them by hand. Use a Japanese beetle trap for large numbers. Follow the manufacturer's directions and hang it away from the pond so it won't attract more beetles to the pond. Neem-based repellents (from neem trees) are also effective.

CROWN ROT

Crown rot is a fungal disease that attacks rhizomes. Water lilies suffering from this disease often lose their central crown and leaves, creating a tell-tale open circle of lily

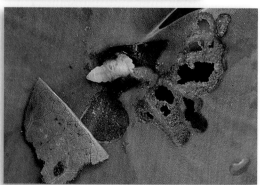

A severe infestation of China mark moths reduces plants to Swiss cheese (top). Unchecked, it can kill plants. The larvae (below) are destructive but easy to control.

LEAF MINERS

Several kinds of larvae generically called leaf miners also attack water lilies. Tiny creatures, they chew or burrow patterns in the leaf surface. If only a few leaves are affected, remove the leaves and throw them away. A larger infestation may be more difficult to treat. Some homeowners report control by dusting the leaves with insecticide. However, some products are toxic to fish and are illegal pad leaves floating on the water. By the time the disease is diagnosed, the entire plant is already infected, so you must remove the rhizome and destroy it. Some gardeners have had success using fungicides, such as metalaxal (Subdue) or thiram, but these are recommended for use only on expensive, difficult-to-replace water lilies.

ANIMAL PESTS

The most frequent animal pests are raccoons and muskrats. Raccoons don't usually eat water plants; instead, they knock them over and tear them apart searching for snails and insect tidbits in the soil. They also enjoy hunting frogs, and love to catch a koi or goldfish that is unlucky enough to swim by. Once in the water, all fish are fair game.

A motion-sensitive impact sprinkler attached to the garden hose, or a net covering the pond, helps deter them. Because raccoons don't like to plunge into deep water, you can protect plants by moving them to the interior of the pond, placing them on bricks to keep them at the proper depth. For more solutions, see page 68.

Muskrats view water lilies and marginal plants as a food source. Emerged water plants, especially cattails and rushes, that aren't eaten will be stripped to the ground and torn to shreds to build a nest. A small muskrat can easily destroy several plants in a single night's work. Muskrat burrows can lead to multiple holes in the liner, collapsed sides, and lots of mud—in other words, a devastated pond. Either place a motion-sensitive impact sprinkler near the pond, or hire someone to legally remove the muskrat.

Occasionally, your water garden may be visited by the neighbor's dog or cat. Deer may also stop by. Although not necessarily harmful to the pond, they can be a nuisance. Homeowners have had to reline entire ponds after a dog's nails punctured the flexible liner. Nearly every gardener has a story of arriving at the garden in the morning ready to work or just enjoy, only to find that the local deer had munched most of the water lily pads and flower buds that would have bloomed that day.

Raccoons can destroy a pond in one night. Attracted to the sound of water or frogs, raccoons topple plants and stones, eat fish and frogs, and chew on water hyacinth.

Short of covering the pond with netting, or placing a fence or other barrier around the property, little can be done to prevent these unsolicited guests from frequenting the water garden. Although a motion-sensitive impact sprinkler might be enough to deter curious animals, even deer, it won't repel a deer that is starving.

Because most pesticides are harmful to fish, you'll need to use materials such as Bt, diatomaceous earth, and insect predators, including dragonflies (bottom left) and predator mites (on cards bottom right), to control pests. Bt does double duty in the pond, preventing mosquitoes from breeding.

CRITTERS

It's the creatures living in and near the pond that transform a picture-perfect water garden into a vibrant, dynamic ecosystem. Children and adults can spend hours watching the acrobatic antics of fish and frogs. It's relaxing, too, to see koi and goldfish gliding effortlessly through the water like little jeweled submarines. With practice, you can even teach the fish to feed from your hand.

Other animals are drawn to the pond by the sight and sound of running water and are fun to observe. Many birds use small ponds as birdbaths. Herons, egrets, and kingfishers search for food. Hummingbirds mist themselves in the spray from a waterfall. Butterflies draw minerals from the wet sand near the edge of the pond; many are attracted to the color and fragrance of flowering water plants as well as to the cooling environment the pond creates.

Animals you probably would rather avoid come, too. Raccoons and opossums visit to

Frogs hunt among lily pads for insects. You can train them to come to you to feed using live crickets. Some will even come hopping out of the pond when they hear the screen door open.

forage for a meal, looking for snails and insects in the soil and fish in the water. If your pond has an earthen bottom, muskrats will think it's a great place to build a home. Snakes warm themselves on the rocks and eat small prey—they are especially attracted to the calls of frogs in the water.

Fish top the list of desirable critters in a pond. Goldfish, koi, bass, bluegill, and rosy red minnows are all popular. How do you choose? Goldfish are usually the easiest to find and prettiest to keep in a backyard pond. Koi are also colorful and popular, as are schools of rosy red minnows. Even tropical fish can be kept in the pond in summer. Not all fish are showy on top. Because you see the fish in the pond only from the top, not from the side as you do in an aquarium, check the fish from all angles before buying.

There are other critters, too. Dragonflies start their lives deep underwater, hiding among decaying leaves at the bottom of the pond. Several varieties of snails call ponds their home. Tadpoles hatch all through the summer as different kinds of frogs and toads use the pond for an amorous getaway. Clams help keep water clear and clean. Even crayfish can live in a backyard pond, although they might consider the plants a full-grown salad bar.

This section offers information and ideas on stocking and caring for animals in your pond, plus some tips on dealing with problems.

Dragonflies are a sign of a healthy pond. They are attracted to ponds with plants. They lay eggs on lily pads, and use upright rushes to get out of the water when they become adults.

Fish can also be trained to eat out of your hand. They can become quite tame and live for many years.

GOLDFISH AND KOI

Fish bring both color and movement to your water garden. They also keep the mosquito population in check. Start with just a few fish, then gradually add more. Goldfish and koi are popular because they are large, colorful fish that are highly visible from above. They are easily trained to take food from your hand. They grow quickly, are generally pest-free, and come in many bright, cheerful colors.

Stocking a pond requires careful planning. Fish can't tolerate the chemicals commonly found in municipal water supplies, so you'll need to neutralize these chemicals before introducing fish to the pond. Also, choose fish with your climate and pool size in mind. Certain species fare better in certain climates and pool depths than in others.

Shubunkin goldfish

The type of fish you stock determines whether you can grow plants in the water garden. Be aware that the diet for both goldfish and koi includes plants, and they can decimate a pond unless you plan for their needs from the start. If the fish are native species, you're safe, at least as far as plant cuisine, because native fish eat other fish. But also for this reason, you can't put native fish in the same pond as goldfish, koi, and tropical fish.

Feed your fish at the same time every day, and you'll soon see them eagerly awaiting you in the pond. Give them as much as they'll eat in 10 minutes or so. Use floating pellets or flakes so that when they're done feeding, you can skim leftover food from the pond. Uneaten fish food will decompose and foul the water, leading to poor water quality as well as algae blooms.

Sarassa comet goldfish

Even if you feed koi and goldfish regularly, they may look for supplemental meals in your plants. Goldfish tend to stay small, up to 10 inches or so in length. Stocking the pond with these smaller fish will keep you from having to worry about your plants.

Koi can grow 3 feet long, and their appetite for plants is huge. To keep large koi, you'll have to take steps to prevent them from eliminating the plants. When koi near 10 inches long, keep an eye on your plants. If the fish overturn potted marginals and destroy other plants, remove the fish and, if possible, find a home for them at your water garden supplier. Don't worry that you'll end up with no fish. By the time they're this large, they've already made more.

Fantail goldfish

If the goldfish are causing problems, the pond has too many fish and too few submerged plants. Rather than removing fish, you can add more plants. Other solutions include constructing a separate, fish-only pond.

With proper management, goldfish and koi make wonderful outdoor pets in the backyard water garden. Because koi have voracious appetites for plants, goldfish may be better choices for small to medium water gardens.

GOLDFISH

Goldfish originated in the Orient and have been prized in China and Japan for centuries. Asian cultures have practiced refined breeding programs to develop many beautiful goldfish forms and varieties. Goldfish are classified by their color, body shape, and finnage. Those known as fancy have long, trailing fins and rounded bodies. Some varieties have unusual eye shapes or forehead flares. Although goldfish can overwinter outdoors, some people bring them indoors for the winter to enjoy their delicate features year-round.

Pearlscale goldfish

The best-known goldfish is probably the comet, which is similar to the orange or red goldfish that many of us had as children. Comets are usually bright orange-red, with long, flowing fins. They have torpedo-shaped bodies and swim quickly, adding a special grace and elegance to the water garden.

TIP

To keep the filtration needs of the pond within the abilities of your filtrator plants and pump filters, follow these guidelines:
Goldfish: Supply at least 5 gallons of water per inch of fish.
Koi: Supply at least 10 gallons of water per inch of fish.
Fish longer than 6 inches need substantially more water.

Yellow and white yamabuki hariwake

There are two other types of comets. Those with red and white markings are known as sarassa comets. Shubunkins are calico-colored. They have a white body with red, blue, orange, yellow, or black markings on their scales.

Other goldfish are fatter and more rounded than comets. Perhaps the best known of these fancy goldfish is the red-cap oranda, with a pearl white body and a red cap, or hat, on the front of its head. All orandas have long, flowing fins; the caudal fin is double and very long and draping.

Orandas come in many colors, including red, black, and white. They may be calico-colored, too, with tricolored scales (Dutch calico oranda), or brown (known as chocolate oranda). Pearlscale has scales that resemble pearly white half-moons.

When you're shopping for fish, you may find some irresistible goldfish with unusual eyes. Bubble-eye goldfish have large sacs that protrude around their eyes. When the eyes extend from the side of the fish's head, the fish is called "telescope" or "dragon-eye." Fish with eyes turned upward are called celestials. Because the eyes and the areas around them are easily damaged, it is not recommended that these types of fish be kept in an outdoor pond.

Gin rin koi

Asagi koi

KOI

Sophisticated relatives of the common carp, koi also have their origins in the Orient. Highly prized and sometimes extremely expensive, koi come in a wide range of colors. Their overall shape, color, and shape of their markings and scales are called their conformation and are the attributes judged in koi shows all over the world.

Koi are classified into categories according to conformation. Distinguishing one type of koi from another requires a keen eye and many years of practice.

The preferred colors are white, red, and black. Blue and silver tones are also possible, as are metallic colors. Butterfly koi, first introduced and raised in the United States, have long, flowing fins. Americans prize them more than koi fanciers in other countries.

One of the most popular categories is the kohaku; these koi are white with red markings. Another favorite is the sanke, which have a white body with red and black markings. Showa have a predominantly black body with red and white markings. Asagi are pale blue with red along their belly and fins. Yamabuki are yellow. Gin rin means the diamond-shaped scales have a sparkly, glittering appearance, regardless of color. Koi with scales that are black in the center are said to be matsuba; those with metallic scales are classified as hikari, and metallic koi of a single color, such as white, are called ogon or hikarimono.

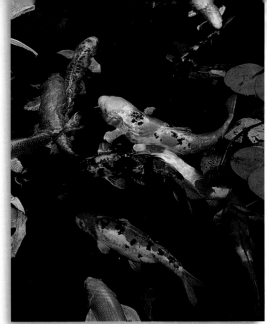

With coloring similar to that of shubunkin goldfish, sanke (the large fish in the center) are among the most popular koi.

This specimen is typical of the hybrid koi that result when fish breed in home ponds.

FISHPOND FILTRATION

Because of their large fish load, koi ponds often must have sophisticated filtering systems. Very large fishponds, such as you may see in parks, need so much external filtration that the system is housed in a small building.

Fishpond filtration can include skimmers and bottom drains, settling tanks, sand filters, ultraviolet sterilizers, diatomaceous earth filters, polishers, biological filters, bead filters, wet-dry filters, aeration towers, up-flow filters, and charcoal filters. Ponds with all of this in place keep the koi or other fish clean and healthy. They are akin to fish swimming pools; the water is so clear that it is transparent, and the fish appear as though they are floating in air.

For most pond owners, such complicated filtration systems are unnecessary. Fish require water that is clean, with perhaps a slight green tint. This more natural design has a charm and beauty all its own, too.

TROPICAL FISH

Tropical fish are good candidates for the pond, whether they're on vacation from the home aquarium or new purchases from the pet shop. When the water temperature warms up into the seventies, tropical fish from indoors benefit from an extended excursion to the pond. With more room and more varied foods to choose from, many even breed and exhibit improved vigor.

Guppies and fancy aquarium fish can be brought outside for a summer vacation. Some even help control mosquitoes and other insects.

Most tropical fish peacefully coexist with goldfish and koi. They may try to eat the same food you feed your goldfish and koi, but it will probably be too large for them to manage, and you will still need to feed them flaked food. Tropical fish also control mosquitoes. They love mosquito larvae, as well as adult mosquitoes that land on the water to lay their eggs.

Small fish such as neon tetras or small guppies can fall prey to dragonfly naiads (immature dragonflies). Brightly colored small (minnow-size) fish also attract the attention of kingfishers. Most small fish can keep their numbers relatively stable, though, by constantly producing offspring. Not all tropical fish coexist peacefully. When purchasing fish, ask the supplier which ones can be combined.

Smaller ponds and container water gardens often have highly fluctuating water temperatures that would be detrimental to koi. But many tropical fish thrive in these

These black mollies, along with orange and green mollies as well as platys, are ideal for small and large water gardens. They form schools without overloading the pond.

conditions. They also are more tolerant of the reduced oxygen levels in small water gardens, unlike koi, which require higher oxygen saturation in the pond water.

Any tropical fish is fine for the pond in terms of adapting, but many look like minnows when seen from above. If you are purchasing fish to add to the pond, find a way to get above them to see how they will look in the pond.

Mollies, swordtails, and platys are probably the best choices for a backyard pond. Resembling miniature goldfish, they come in many sizes, shapes, and colors. They reproduce well, are easy to care for, and accept a wide range of habitats. With colors in bright red, orange, yellow, green, black, and white, they are highly visible. Relatively wide-bodied, they are easy to see in the pond. Guppies are difficult to see in the pond, because they are generally gray-tan on top. Remember to bring tropical fish indoors when pond water dips below 70° F.

NATIVE FISH

Bluegill

Raising native fish in the backyard pond may be a novel idea to some, but it has been done successfully for many years, especially among those who are conservation-minded. It's sensible, too, when you stop to think about it. Native fish are accustomed to the local climate and weather conditions. They prefer the area's flora and fauna for their daily dinner. With the proper protection, they will withstand both the winter freeze and the summer heat and humidity.

Game fish such as bass, perch, crappie, bluegill, and catfish are all predatory fish. They eat the other fish in the water and are not suitable for a pond with ornamental fish such as koi or goldfish. When they're all mixed together, the less aggressive fish (including the koi and goldfish) will tend to "disappear" or become injured, no matter how small the predatory fish may be.

Native fish come in all sizes, shapes, and colors. In a deep pond, the family anglers can practice their casting talents for bass, bluegill, even pike. In a shallow pond, the children can enjoy watching the schooling habits of tiny sunfish, also known as bream.

Some of the more common or popular native fish include top minnows, shiners, and killifish. Top minnows are long, thin, colorful fish that consume several times their weight in mosquito larvae. They are called top minnows because they live in the top few inches of water along the pond surface.

Sunfish are more rounded than top minnows. Living deeper in the pond, the various species of sunfish are brightly colored on their sides and often have different temperaments. Some are outgoing and gregarious; others are quite shy.

Keeping native fish in your backyard pond is an ideal way to appreciate and learn about your local environment and habitat. Make sure to find out from the appropriate wildlife authorities which species are allowed and which are protected. Learn about the fish species' particular needs for food and water conditions so they will be safe and thrive in your pond. You might even be able to collect native fish from local waters. Check with the natural resources department in your area and follow all regulations regarding licenses and netting.

Native fish, such as this largemouth bass, grow quickly in a water garden. If included in your pond, be aware that they eat other fish.

PRAISE FOR THE MOSQUITO FISH

Although water attracts many desirable creatures, it draws one insect that no one enjoys—the mosquito. These pesky biters come to the water to lay their eggs, which hatch into younglings that live in the water for a while before they transform into adult, winged mosquitoes. Most species of mosquitoes prefer still, even stagnant, water, but some will lay their eggs in moving water, including a stream in your backyard. Mosquito fish (*Gambusia* spp.) are considered an effective pest control method to rid the water of mosquito larvae. You need only a few in a normal-size backyard pond. In southern Florida, mosquito fish are used as a nonchemical method of mosquito control. In fact, the fish are released by planes flying over the marshes and Everglades. The fish make a free fall to the water below, where they live and breed, consuming large quantities of mosquito larvae.

FROGS, TURTLES, AND OTHER CREATURES

Frogs are the most musical addition to the pond. During spring, the breeding calls of mating frogs can be quite loud. If you get too many, bless a park pond with the extras.

If you notice frogs or toads in or near your pond, you are in for a treat. Some homeowners have been able to tame the visitors by feeding them live bait such as crickets or earthworms. It's delightful to sit near the pond and listen to their calls, trying to distinguish each species by its unique sound.

Frog and toad tadpoles appear in the water garden in late spring and intermittently throughout the summer. The adults' early-spring mating calls are the first signal of the tadpoles' later arrival. Some tadpoles, such as those for spring peepers, or tree frogs, are less than a quarter-inch long. They last in the water for a few days or weeks, then transform into frogs. Other frog species spawn tadpoles that live longer. Bullfrog tadpoles, for example, spend up to two summers as tadpoles before changing into full-grown frogs.

Once grown, adult green frogs and bullfrogs live in the pond year-round. Leopard frogs spend some time in or near the water but spend most of their time on dry land.

Frogs require little attention from the pond owner. Use plants around the edge of the pond that will provide shade and cover for them, such as arrowhead or sedges. Before mowing the lawn, walk the area around the pond to shoo frogs back into the water. In cold climates, you can build a mound of twigs and leaves near the edge of the pond so the toads will have a place to burrow during the winter. Frogs will bury themselves in the pond mud for the winter.

Not all frogs are neighborly inhabitants in the water garden. Although green frogs and leopard frogs eat only insects, bullfrogs are voracious and omnivorous. Adult bullfrogs

M any types of amphibians are attracted to water gardens. They are a sign of a healthy, balanced pond ecosystem and provide hours of enjoyment for you and your family.

FROGS

Some frogs come to live in the water; others just visit to sample the local insect fare. Most toads spend only enough time in the water to lay their eggs, leaving afterward for their preferred terrestrial surroundings. They, too, enjoy munching on the many insects drawn to the water and will do their part in eliminating any mosquitoes around the pond.

Someday your pond will have tadpoles. If their numbers are too great, net them and deposit them in a nearby stream or pond. Some tadpoles may stay in the pond for several seasons.

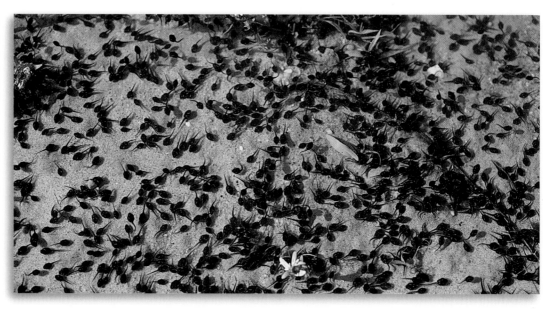

have been known to eat goldfish and koi. They will snatch small birds that come to drink or bathe. It's best to relocate a full-grown bullfrog to a natural body of water, unless you have a very large pond and don't mind losing a few small fish to its rapacious appetite.

TURTLES

Some species of turtles are water-loving amphibians that are delightful, but hungry, pond inhabitants. Red-eared sliders, painted turtles, and snapping turtles all enjoy the water in a backyard pond. They also consider your favorite koi or goldfish as prime fillet for dinner, with snails as the hors d'oeuvres. Turtles love to snip water lily pads and oxygenator plants from the bottom of the pond. And snapping turtles live up to their name if disturbed.

If you want turtles in your water garden, create a separate pond just for them. You will have to build a fence or other enclosure to prevent them from wandering away. To learn how to properly care for turtles throughout the year, check with a herpetology club in your area or look on the Internet. Also ask your state's natural resources department whether keeping a turtle is allowed in your area. Many new laws are being passed that restrict or prohibit catching and keeping native fauna, including turtles.

SNAILS

Snails help keep down algae. However, they are not the turbocharged algae cleaners that some folks make them out to be. If you added enough snails to keep your pond algae-free, there would be little else in the water. It takes at least one snail for every 1 to 2 square feet of water surface. A 10×10-foot pond, 2 feet deep, would need 100 to 200 large snails.

Carefully choose which snails you add to the pond. Avoid Columbian ramshorn and apple snails. They eat water plants, especially water lilies. Japanese snails, northern ramshorn, which are about the size of a dime, and trapdoor snails leave plants alone, preferring instead surplus fish food, fish excrement, and the algae that grow like a green lawn on the sides of your pond.

SHELLFISH

Clams and mussels are ideal in water gardens. They are eager cleaners of pond water, filtering up to 200 gallons a day and combing

Turtles like to wander off. If you move a pet turtle outdoors for the summer, build a fence in a protected area by the pond. Remember, raccoons eat small turtles, and turtles eat fish. You'll need to provide protection for all.

out the green-pea-soup algae. They provide a fine service to the pond because of their natural filtering abilities, and they live for many years. They are easy to care for, too. Just place them in a pot or tray of soft sand at least 6 inches deep. They will bury themselves with just the tip sticking out.

It is now illegal in some areas to remove a freshwater clam or mussel from the wild to place in your pond, so check with the natural resources department in your area to become aware of local restrictions.

Crayfish tend to be plant eaters as well as scavengers, and so are not recommended for ornamental ponds. If you add one, give it a place to hide, such as a clay tile or rock pile.

DRAGONFLIES

Dragonflies and damselflies are so adept at snatching mosquitoes on the wing that they are known as mosquito hawks. They consume up to 200 mosquitoes a day. More than 450 species of dragonflies exist in North America alone. They usually find ponds themselves, so there is no need to introduce them to yours. Even so, many water garden suppliers and mail-order sources carry the juvenile forms of dragonflies and damselflies.

These juveniles may take a year or more to mature. They are carnivorous at this stage, living underwater and feeding on insects as well as very small fish. The adults live for three to four months and will guard a territory around the pond against others of the same species. Adults lay eggs on the underside of water lily leaves or directly on the surface of the water. These eggs hatch in late summer, and the juveniles overwinter in the pond, even in cold climates.

STOCKING THE POND

Local and mail-order sources of fish and other living pond creatures abound, so search out a reputable dealer—ideally, someone you know and trust. When working with a local supplier, you have the opportunity to check out the animals before buying. Look for fish that are alert and swim freely in the tank. Avoid fish that swim sideways or those that seem to have trouble navigating. All animals should be free of spots, sores, or ulcers, and fish fins should be clean and full, not tattered or worn.

SAFELY TRANSPORTING FISH

Each of the water creatures you buy for your pond should have its own bag with plenty of air inside. Keep the animals cool and take them right home.

Bringing home new fish can be a stressful time for them and you. To keep problems to a minimum, plan well. Fish are usually transported in plastic bags; place the bag in a polystyrene box for the journey home, because it will act as an insulator and reduce changes in water temperature. A sturdy cardboard box will suffice. Keep the fish cool and in the shade. If traveling by car, don't put the bag in the trunk or in direct sunlight, or it will overheat.

It's best to take the fish straight home. The longer they are in the bag, the more stress they have to endure. If the fish will be in the bag for more than a half hour or so, have the store add extra oxygen to the bag, otherwise the fish will use up the available oxygen during transport. For extra-long trips, it's advisable to add a nontoxic disinfectant to the transport water. Some suppliers even add a medication that acts as a mild sedative.

MAIL-ORDER CRITTERS

If ordering by mail, request the fastest shipping possible—overnight is best. If you're buying snails or other aquatic animals as well as fish, ask that each type of creature be shipped in a different bag with oxygen and water. That way, they can't bump into each other or attack one another during the trip.

Snails are sometimes shipped with plant material in their container, but this isn't the best shipment method. Plants use oxygen when they're in the dark, so when they're in the transport box, they will use up the oxygen the snails need.

Tadpoles are usually shipped like fish, in bags. Offer them plenty of food—crushed, dry fish food, or small, flaked fish food—as soon as they arrive. Any interruption in their food supply may trigger their development into frogs, and you don't want them to transform into frogs right away, especially if you bought them to eat algae or to scavenge in the pond.

ADDING CRITTERS TO YOUR POND

As a general rule, it's best not to introduce fish or other creatures to the pond during excessively hot or freezing weather, or during early spring when temperatures fluctuate greatly. All of these conditions stress the animals, causing them to succumb to disease or illness and ultimately leading to their demise.

When you add a new fish to the pond, you must acclimate it gradually because of its swim bladder (an internal organ that controls buoyancy, which can expand and burst if subjected to extreme changes in water temperature). To do this, float the unopened bag in the pond for a few

minutes. Do not release the fish into the pond until the temperature of the water in the bag is within 2° F of the pond temperature.

Floating the bag helps to even out the water temperature. If the bag is in the sun, put a light-colored, damp towel over it so that the rays from the sun don't heat up the bag. After a few minutes, use a net to gently remove the fish from the bag and place it in the pond.

If your new fish isn't in a bag but is in a bucket or other container, add some of your pond water gradually to the container so the fish becomes acclimated to the pond water temperature. Then gently net the fish and move it to the pond. Very large fish can be lifted with a special sling net that will lessen the possibility that the fish will flip out or thrash around, hurting itself in the process.

Snails don't need to be acclimated to the water because they don't have a swim bladder. Tadpoles also don't have a swim bladder, so they will acclimate to the new pond temperature without needing to be floated.

Unless you know that the bag water the fish, snails, and tadpoles arrive in is safe, it's best not to add it to your pond water. Water from another pond may contain chemicals or diseases that aren't present in your own pond, and you don't want to introduce them. Fish transported over long distances are often sent in water that has been specially treated to keep the fish sedated and medicated. Don't taint your pond by adding this water.

Some authorities recommend that new fish be treated and/or quarantined before they are added to the general fish population. One precaution is to treat the fish by "dipping" them in a low-salt solution or a special chemical mixture such as formalin for the most common forms of fish diseases. These measures may be appropriate if you already have many fish in your pond. Follow the manufacturer's directions very closely with respect to any chemical treatment, and set up a separate quarantine tank for such treatment, leaving your main pond unaffected.

Feed fish once or twice a day with floating pellets or stick food. Most fish readily adjust to this type of food. Remove any food they don't eat so it doesn't foul the water.

When stocking fish, place their unopened bag in the pond so they can adjust to the water temperature.

OUTWITTING PROBLEMS

S everal kinds of animals can be a threat to your pond inhabitants, especially to koi and goldfish. Besides protecting them from predators, a good pond keeper also checks the fish regularly for illness or disease. Some even use a quarantine tank to hold, treat, and inspect any new fish before introducing them to the pond, to make sure the new fish do not have a disease or illness that could spread to the rest of the fish population. This is one area where an ounce of prevention is surely worth a pound of cure.

PREDATORS

One of the most common pests is the raccoon (for others, see page 57). It will come around dusk, or in the early hours of the morning to feed on insects and small snails. Raccoons eat live fish, so they will try to catch those in your pond. Slow-moving fish, such as fancy goldfish, are easy prey and need particular protection.

One way to deter raccoons is to design the pond so they don't have easy access to the fish in the first place. Raccoons like to wade in shallow water and are reluctant to venture into water that's more than 6 to 8 inches deep. Shallow ledges invite the raccoon to wade into the water, knocking over potted plants and generally wreaking havoc. So build the pond more than a foot deep,

Streamers across a pond help scare off birds. They are a quick solution, but not a permanent one; the birds may adjust to their presence after a few weeks.

Automatic scarecrow sprinklers help deter herons, deer, raccoons, and possums, however, they're not a 100-percent control. Use a couple of sprinklers to protect a large pond.

without shallow shelves along the edges. Locate marginal plants away from the edges and support them at the correct depth on bricks. These measures are also effective against possums, which will search the pond for food, whether insects, frogs, or fish.

Herons and egrets are also fish predators. Unlike raccoons, they are not dissuaded by straight pond sides or deep water. Various products are offered as "heron guards," with varying degrees of success. These include an artificial but real-looking heron that can be placed on a post along the edge of the pond. Because birds are territorial, they will not approach when they see another of their kind already near the pond—until they realize that the bird is just a decoy.

Large blankets of netting, such as that used to protect fruit trees from birds, will keep raccoons, possums, herons, and egrets at bay. It's effective but unattractive. If you use it, float a large ball in the pond so the netting does not sink. If the only concern is night-marauding raccoons and opossums, the netting can be placed over the pond in late evening and removed in the morning. If birds are the culprits, the netting will have to remain over the pond day and night.

A 6-inch-tall, low-voltage electric fence also can prevent access to raccoons, opossums, muskrats, and dogs. Crisscrossing the pond with string or clear fishing line is effective against certain birds, including Canada geese. The birds land on the lawn near the pond, but the string prevents them from reaching the water. Unable to traverse the fishing line "fence," they become disenchanted and leave the pond alone.

Perhaps the most effective deterrent is an impact sprinkler with a motion-sensitive device attached to the garden hose. When activated, it sprays a strong jet of water in a wide circle. Startled by the spray, the intruder runs or flies away. The sprinkler can be left on all the time to ward off many sorts of pests. Remember to turn it off, so you and your friends don't get soaked when you go to feed the fish or admire the waterfall!

DISEASES AND PARASITES

Goldfish and koi may fall victim to several parasitic or bacterial infections. These may occur because a new fish, infected with a disease, has been introduced to the pond. Many times, however, it's simply something outside the water gardener's control. For example, several kinds of parasites and bacteria occur naturally in pond water. Although present, they generally don't harm fish because the fishes' immune system wards off any attack. When the immune system becomes compromised, fish may become sick.

The most effective way to ensure the fish stay healthy is to practice good pond maintenance. Keep the water clean. Don't allow uneaten fish food, dead leaves, or other organic debris to remain in the pond. Test the water periodically for nitrite, ammonia, and nitrate levels with an accurate test kit. If you refill the pond with municipal water, use chloramine remover and dechlorinator to remove chlorine, chloramines, and heavy metals from the water.

One common fish ailment is anchor worm, caused by a parasite that attaches to the fish's skin, leaving a small red mark. The parasite may be visible. Remove it with tweezers and treat the wound with a small swab of a topical medication, such as Betadine. Small ulcers or lesions may appear, especially in spring when fish are spawning. These, too, may be treated with Betadine or a similar medication.

Some illnesses become noticeable because they change fish behavior. Fish gasping near the water surface, especially near a waterfall or fountain, may signal oxygen depletion, nitrite toxicity, or gill flukes (flatworm parasites). Nitrite toxicity is more common in summer when the pond water temperature soars, causing a sudden rise in nitrite levels. Lower the nitrite level and add oxygen with a partial water change and increased aeration.

Fish that suddenly swim very quickly, scraping themselves against the pond sides, may have "ich," a common parasitic infection that manifests itself as small white dots on the fish's skin. Ask your dealer for medication.

TREATING ILLNESSES

Whatever the ailment and the treatment, closely follow the manufacturer's directions whenever you use a medication. Don't use more than the recommended dosage or use it more often than what is called for. If the disease is contagious, move the ill fish to a quarantine tank to protect the rest of the fish in your pond, or follow label directions for treating the entire fish population.

Consult your fish supplier to help you diagnose the disease and select the proper treatment for your area and conditions. Many diseases are seasonal; temperature and climate changes can cause an outbreak. If your fish are ill with a disease, it is likely that other local pond owners are having similar

difficulties. Talking to a reputable supplier as well as neighboring water gardeners will bring common problems and cures to light.

QUARANTINE

When fish fall ill or develop signs that they may be ailing, it's wise to place them in quarantine to treat them. This hospital pond should be completely independent of the main pond. Place it several feet away from your main pond so water spray won't drift from the hospital pond and infect the main pond. Don't use the same pump or filter, or even the same nets, in both the quarantine pond and your water garden. Bleach or chlorine are the best disinfectants.

The quarantine pond should have all the attributes of a regular pond. Depending on its size and the type, number, and size of fish in it, the hospital pond should have a pump to circulate the water and a filtration system to clean the water. It may be necessary to place a net over the pond to prevent fish from jumping out; koi especially are prone to jumping in an effort to escape their new confines.

Never buy a sick fish, no matter how beautiful, with the thought that you'll be able to treat it. Ulcer disease, such as this, is a serious condition that needs treatment and vigilance until cured.

A well-designed pond with the right number of fish for the amount of water and enough plants to support them requires little care. If you would like water gardening to be a more intense hobby, try a koi pond. Not only can you compete with other fanciers for the showiest koi, but they offer plenty of opportunities to "primp" the pond.

TAKING CARE OF THE POND

A well-designed water garden should take minimal time to maintain. Unless you have a very large water feature or a fish-only pond, you'll spend about an hour or less each week to feed fish, groom plants, and monitor water quality. When estimating the amount of time to budget for garden pool maintenance, plan on about 10 minutes per thousand gallons of water per week.

Completely emptying and cleaning the water feature on a regular basis isn't necessary, nor is it advisable. In fact, frequent emptying and cleaning can cause more harm than good. It can injure your fish as they try to adjust to varying water temperatures and conditions. It can destroy and wash away beneficial bacteria, which can take days, even weeks, to reestablish. Unless the pond is very dirty from too many fish or too many decaying leaves in the water, most ponds need to be drained, cleaned, and refilled only once every few years.

Fishponds require quite a bit of care to keep fish wastes from fouling the water and to maintain fish health. Plan on spending extra time cleaning filters, which remove the wastes, skimming debris from the water, and ensuring the pumps that aerate and recirculate water are working.

If your water garden takes too much time to maintain, it may have a fundamental problem in its design or construction or in the ratio of plants, fish, and water. It's better to correct the basic problem instead of spending hours each week fixing its side effects. In the long run, you'll save time and money. If you can't determine the source of the problem, consult a professional water garden specialist.

As long as the pond has no problems, you'll have a burst of chores in spring—dividing plants and returning them to their spots in the pond, removing dead foliage, and so on—and in fall—readying the pond for winter—and just a little grooming each week in between. The few extra hours in spring and fall will save many hours of headaches throughout the summer. Your water will stay clearer, your fish healthier, and your plants greener and more floriferous.

FUNDAMENTALS

Water splashing from a fountain aerates the pond, keeping it fresh and free of anaerobic bacteria, which thrive in oxygen-depleted environments and produce rank odors.

If salt and fish wastes have built up in the pond, drain off about 10 percent of the water, then refill. A biological filter can help skim off some of the wastes.

Spreading bird netting over the pond in fall is a simple way to catch leaves and make cleanup easier. Hold the netting in place with bricks or stones.

Ponds in the wild contain a complex network of checks and balances that generally maintain pond health without help. Garden ponds have the same network but, being artificial, require your assistance. If your pond is out of balance, it will give you signals: bad smells, fish dying or gasping for breath at the surface, dark or green water, and stunted and diseased plants. Here's how to help keep your garden pond healthy.

USE ALL THE ELEMENTS: Plants and other pond life work together. Fish are not required in the water garden, but they do consume mosquito larvae and add lively interest to the pond. Floating plants provide shade, and they cool and filter the water and control algae. Submerged plants are also filters, and they feed fish as well as create shelter and spawning areas for them. Use one bunch of submerged plants for every 2 square feet of pond surface. Also, stock the pond with snails, which feed on the algae.

KNOW YOUR WATER: Invest in a kit for testing pond water. They're inexpensive, and a number of types are available. Test for ammonia and nitrite levels when you first fill your pond, then periodically thereafter, particularly if fish look stressed or are dying. If the pond develops a chemical problem, a partial water change, described below, will help lower ammonia and nitrite levels.

KEEP THE POND FILLED: Don't let the pond evaporate—a drop of an inch or more below the normal water level starts to create unhealthy concentrations of salts and minerals and exposes the liner to deteriorating UV rays.

When you add water, fill the pond with just a trickle from the hose (keep it at the bottom of the pond) to allow fish and other pond life to adapt to the gradual changes in temperature and pH. Add no more than 10 to 20 percent of the total volume at any one time or the fish could go into shock. If using municipal water, add chlorine remover to the pond whenever you top it off.

Partially change the water when needed. Although it's best to keep the pond filled, over time—even with refills—salt and waste

materials build up in the water. To freshen the pond, drain it by about 10 percent of its capacity, preferably by drawing water from the bottom, where concentrations of harmful substances are highest. Then refill it as described. It's best to do this right before a rain, so rainfall can replace at least some of the water.

PROVIDE AERATION: Whether from a fountain or waterfall, splashing water keeps the pond well-oxygenated, which is essential for supporting fish. Oxygenated water also stays fresh, warding off foul-smelling bacteria that thrive in a low-oxygen environment.

REMOVE LEAVES AND DEBRIS: Debris decomposes and fouls water if not removed. Skim leaves, fallen petals, and other floating plant matter from the bottom and surface of the pond with a net or by hand.

Pinch off yellowing and dying leaves. In autumn, put netting over the pond to catch falling leaves, or make skimming the pond a daily routine. In late fall, when you remove the pump for the winter, make sure the water is free of debris before the pond ices over.

KEEP IT UNDER CONTROL: If fish numbers get out of hand, give some away. Regularly thin aggressive plants, and divide overgrown plants so no one element takes over.

CONSIDER A FILTER: If the garden pond has continuing problems with debris, too much light, or excessive fish waste, consider adding a biological filter to the pond setup.

PREVENT RUNOFF: When fertilizing or applying other chemicals to the lawn and plants surrounding your garden pond, don't let the materials run off or trickle into the water. They can be toxic to fish and may promote algae growth in the water.

FEED FISH PROPERLY: Feeding too much or too often fouls the water and necessitates a larger filter. Feed fish only when they are ravenous, then give them only as much as they can eat in about 10 minutes.

ALGAE

Many garden ponds, especially during the first two to three weeks after they're constructed or cleaned, have excess algae. Most have an algae bloom each spring, too, as the pond regroups from winter. But as your water lilies and floating plants grow and begin to shade the water surface and compete with algae for light, the water should clear. If it doesn't, the pond may need help.

Certain kinds of algae are good for ponds, however. Smooth algae, for example, grow on the liner and on pots. It is a sign of a healthy pond and gives a water garden an attractive patina, making it look as though it has been there awhile. Smooth algae growth is called

a passive filter because it removes nutrients that nourish less desirable algae.

Free-floating, filamentous, and tufted algae (sometimes called blanketweed or string algae), as well as floating phytoplankton algae, are undesirable. These grow in long, ropy, dark green colonies and can turn water green and murky. In severe cases, they coat and choke out other plants and stress fish.

CONTROLLING ALGAE

Algae grows rapidly in warm water, so keep your pond filled, particularly in hot weather. Deep ponds warm up more slowly than shallow ones.

Remove filamentous algae, which looks like floating seaweed, from the water surface by hand or with a stick, rake, or toilet brush. If it forms on rocks or waterfalls, turn off the pump and let the algae dry. Then scrape and brush it off. If that doesn't work, rewet the algae and sprinkle it with noniodized table salt, such as pickling and canning salt. Leave for several hours, then brush off. Salt, as long as it is used only rarely and in moderation, kills algae but doesn't harm fish.

Hydrogen peroxide also destroys algae that clings to rocks and does not harm fish or plants. Spray it on algae, which will turn white and can be easily removed with a little scrub brush. Pond snails, too, are algae eaters.

Use algaecides as a last resort. They might stunt the plant growth.

If algae occur regularly, a biological filter may be in order, or a UV clarifier, which can defend your pond against algae. A properly sized UV clarifier-pump combination will also kill harmful bacteria, viruses, and fungi that attack fish.

String algae can help keep water crystal clear but can quickly take over if too many nutrients are available. Simply remove excess algae with a toilet bowl brush tied to a pole.

KEEPING THE POND CLEAN

Cleaning a pond is a chore you'll need to perform only once in a while. It helps keep a pond healthy by reducing algae and other problems.

Signs that your pond should be cleaned include overgrown plants and a several-inch-thick layer of decomposing debris on the bottom. Remember, this should occur only every three to four years.

Late summer to early fall is the best time to clean ponds. If the pond has fish, do the work on a cool day, which is easier on fish, at least a month before winter sets in to give the fish enough time to recover. In warm climates, wait until plants go dormant and the water temperature is around 60° F.

First, drain the pond. You can bail the water, or if you have a submersible pump, replace the output piping with a hose. Run the hose out of the pond and siphon the water.

Partially empty the pond to make it easier to catch fish. Net them and place them in a bucket of pond water. After catching a few, transfer them to a 30-gallon trash can or an untreated (for algae) child's wading pool in the shade or a cool indoor room. This holding pen should be filled the day before with half-and-half pond and fresh water, treated to remove chlorine and chloramines. Cover the holding pen so the fish won't jump out. Don't feed the fish at this time. If they are going to be held for more than an hour, put an aerator in the container.

Continue to remove water until only several inches remain in the bottom of the pond. Then stop pumping and check the muck for small fish and frogs, tadpoles, and other animals. Put these in the container also.

Next, remove the plants. Take care that their foliage remains wet or at least damp, so they survive their out-of-water experience. You can wrap foliage and pots in wet newspaper and set plants in the shade, or submerge them in the wading pool or in buckets of water.

Bail the remaining water and pour it onto flower beds and the rest of the landscape. Don't pour it down a drain; it will clog the plumbing. Scoop mud from the pond bottom, taking care not to damage the liner. Dump the mud on the compost pile.

Once the pond is empty, hose it down. Use a soft brush to clean the sides of the liner. Scrubbing also removes beneficial bacteria and helpful algae, so don't scrub too thoroughly. After hosing down the pond, remove the dirty water. Next, fill the pond about halfway and add the plants.

Fill the pond, preparing the water in the same way as for the pool's first stocking, with chlorine and chloramine removers, if necessary. Check the fish for disease, and treat them accordingly. Then gently place them in plastic bags, inflating and sealing the bags. Float the bags and release the fish as described on pages 66 and 67. Another method is to gradually add fresh pond water to the holding pen. When the container's water temperature is within 2° F of the pond's, release the fish.

WINTER CARE

In regions with mild winters, care of the garden pond consists of little more than an occasional check on the pond and its inhabitants. However, in cold parts of the country, you'll need to protect the water feature itself as well as its inhabitants.

First, the water feature. Ponds made of masonry or other porous material can crack, especially if above ground. If there's any danger of the pond freezing solid, where the entire depth of water turns to ice, drain it using a pump or siphon hose. Also drain fountains. Ponds made from flexible or pre-formed liner or earth-bottomed ponds don't need to be drained. A properly constructed in-ground concrete pond that is filled should also be able to withstand freezing.

Instead of draining the pond, you can install a stock tank deicer to keep it from freezing. However, deicers can be expensive to operate, costing as much as $100 a month in electricity in some areas. You can reduce your bill by turning on the deicer only when the ice is 4 to 6 inches thick, or once a week for a day or so. The purpose of the deicer is to keep a hole thawed in the ice, not to keep the pond completely ice-free.

In regions where the air temperature doesn't drop below –10° F, use an air pump with an air stone to keep water moving enough to prevent freezing. Where the temperature stays above –20° F, a water pump will keep the pond from freezing solid.

In cold-weather climates, lift nonhardy water plants and ones in small water gardens that freeze solid. Store them indoors.

Both methods, however, work best in ponds of 1,000 gallons or more because large bodies of water freeze more slowly than small ones.

In these large ponds, hardy fish and plants can survive the winter if the ice doesn't completely cover the pond. If it does, oxygen can't move into the water, and harmful gases are trapped in it. Drill thick ice with an ice auger. Never smash ice because the vibrations can shock and even kill the fish.

In mild climates where ice never forms more than 2 inches thick, you can prevent damaging water expansion by floating a piece of plastic foam in the pond. It should be at least a foot square and 2 inches thick.

If the pond is small and likely to freeze solid, move fish and plants indoors. After frost kills the foliage of hardy plants, cut off dead stems to within a couple of inches of the soil. Store the pots in a cool, not freezing, spot in trash bags with moist newspapers so they stay damp and dark until the pond becomes free of daytime ice. Overwinter fish in aquariums, or give them away and buy new fish in spring.

Plan on doing at least one recurring task: cleaning the filter. You may have to rinse the pad every few days to remove all particulate matter and keep it from clogging the pump.

PROJECTS

Colorful fish, splashing water, elegant blossoms. The plans on these pages can help bring the beauty of a water garden home to your yard.

The most successful water gardens follow a plan and have a design that holds together the entire project. The plan and design need to be integrated with the contours and style of the overall landscape and with the gardener's individual lifestyle.

The best plan, therefore, will always reflect a balance of both practical and aesthetic elements. For example, the size and shape of your water garden should conform not only to the scale of your yard but also to the amount of time and funds you can devote to the maintenance of its plants and wildlife.

If you have less than an hour each week to devote to caring for your pond, consider a small installation, even if you have a large backyard. Similarly, if your schedule allows you to enjoy your pond only in the evening and on weekends, your best bet might be to have a "moon garden," with tropical water lilies and other plants that bloom at night.

If your primary interest is attracting birds and butterflies, you'll need to include design features such as a sandy butterfly beach or a shallow area at the pond edge that will act as a birdbath. Moisture-loving plants will bring butterflies to the pond. Pickerel weed and water snowball (*Gymocoronis spilanthoides*) attract butterflies.

Families with young children might take comfort in the safety, and beauty, of a bog garden. Container gardens are also perfect around children or in small urban spaces. Even a pot that's sealed, then filled with water makes a wonderful container pond.

On the following pages are two case studies of a large bog garden, plus ideas for a container water garden. Study them for inspiration to apply to your own backyard or patio.

A LARGE POND

This large water garden is installed in a quarter-acre backyard. The goals of the homeowner were to install as big and natural a pond as possible, given certain site limitations that affected the pond's location, shape, and size.

THE POND TAKES SHAPE

The slope limited the usable space for a water garden to about 35 feet in the area between the house and the rear of the yard. Because the owner did not want to go to the expense of digging into the slope and erecting a substantial retaining wall, the natural choice was to build the pond with its length spanning the width of the yard. Hence, even with a 42-foot stream, the main body of the pond's 31-foot length fits comfortably, without seeming cramped, into the 75-foot-long yard, and the short stream terminates toward the rear of the yard with 10 feet to spare to the incline of the slope.

A large oak tree prohibited pond excavation in the area of its roots, but by roughly centering the points on the pond where the streams empty into it, the design helps integrate the garden naturally with the tree and other existing features.

Sun and shade patterns also had an effect on the placement of this garden. At the rear of the property, a line of tall trees limits the sun and casts the pond in dappled shade. In addition, a good portion of the yard is shaded in the afternoon by the profile of the garage. To make sure the sun-loving water plants didn't grow up in shadows, the initial pond location was moved to the right to catch more afternoon light.

Personal factors also affected design elements. The 42-foot stream provided a location for a waterfall, for its delightful music and because it attracts birds. It also houses a biological filter, which keeps the water healthy for its finned inhabitants. The waterfall was located where a window in the family room could frame a view of it. The pond's western edge terminates under the deck, allowing more intimate contact with the water (dangling feet in it, for example), and makes it feel like a lakeside dock.

The under-deck location also hides a filter, called a skimmer box (see "How a Skimmer Box Works," page 78), as well as underwater lighting and its accompanying electrical lines. A 14-foot stream allows complete circulation of the pond water from one end to the other.

Workers laid out the conformation of the pond with garden hose and finalized the angle

Located where it is framed by the windows in the family room, this pond seems to be as much a part of the interior landscape as it is of the backyard. Having a focal point at the end of the pond— the waterfall, here—makes the view especially appealing.

of view of the waterfalls from all the windows in the house by positioning and repositioning wheelbarrows. The final contour was painted on the ground for excavation. PVC piping (2-inch flexible PVC for the pump wiring and pump return lines) was laid first, so soil from the hole could hide the piping and create a berm high enough for the waterfalls (4 feet at the upper pond, 18 inches where the streams empty into the pond). Included in the excavation were the siting of components for the filtration system.

The pond is shallow along its edges, with intermittent 6-inch shelves for marginals. One of these shelves begins at the point where the long stream empties into the pond and continues for about 8 feet, where it then tapers back to the pond edge. At the end of this shelf, the water is 18 inches deep, which

Shortly after planting, the "bones" of a pond are still starkly visible. This is a good stage to visit ponds for ideas; it's when you can see how they're built. The filter for this pond is under the deck.

A LARGE POND
continued

Plants fill the beds, from typical landlubbers— hostas, junipers, and astilbe—to water babies, such as taro and arrowhead.

The owners used wheelbarrows as stand-ins for the waterfalls as they decided on the falls' placement. They built berms for the waterfalls from excavated soil and fieldstone.

The pond is comprised of a main body, a stream and two waterfalls. Pavers and decking give a sharp edge to the informal garden.

allows submerged plants to be brought right to the pond edge.

In the center of its main body, and in a roughly defined circle, the pond is 30 inches deep to allow fish a place of refuge and, in winter, protection from cold water. The sides of this central area are tapered up to an 18-inch shelf, which is home to lotus.

A combination of medium and large boulders (some 6 to 12 inches in diameter, others 18 to 24 inches), placed both underwater and partially submerged, holds the pond's liner in place and is the first step in establishing the pond's natural style. The boulders are stacked against the walls of the pond, and a layer of ¼- to 2-inch river rock completes the protection over its remaining bottom surface. All in all, the pond contains 7 tons of aqua blue stone, 2 tons of 18- to 24-inch accent boulders, and 5 tons of 6- to 12-inch Wisconsin mountain granite.

At the rear edge of the pond are miniature cattail and iris, whose 3- to 4-foot height provides a vertical backdrop for the smaller

aquatic plants in front but does not obscure the view of the tree line at the rear of the yard. These smaller plants grow in pockets formed from small stones (small rock pots, as it were) without soil. Lilies lounge in the sunlit sections of the pond, and pickerel weed holds down the shaded edges. In the streams there are more miniature cattails and iris, along with forget-me-nots and aquatic mint. Water hyacinth dots the upper pond.

Koi populate this pond without feeding on the lilies or the other plants. Bought when they were 4 to 5 inches long, they have become habituated to regular feeding by the owner and thus don't seek a supplemental diet from the plants.

HOW A SKIMMER BOX WORKS

A skimmer box, usually made from fiberglass or plastic, houses a pump and filter pads. It draws water into its opening, where the pads screen debris from the water surface. Skimmers are designed to sit in the ground at the edge of the pond, where you can hide them with rocks, a deck, or other landscape features. Water from the skimmer is discharged through piping to the other end of the pond, where it is further filtered biologically. This cycle ensures complete circulation of the water. Small header pools are often placed at this discharge end of the pond, to hold the water so it can spill in a waterfall into the main pond. This simple design incorporates the two forms of filtration—mechanical and biological—that most ponds need to be healthy and attractive.

THE POND'S UNDERPINNINGS

Although wet newspaper makes an excellent underlayment for almost any pond, the owner used geotextile fabric in this one, followed by 45-mil EPDM liner. EPDM is more costly in the short run but carries a 20-year guarantee. You can use any flexible liner.

Still water in a pond can become stagnant, and a well-stocked koi pond requires filtration to remove wastes. This pond uses two skimmer boxes and two biological filters to keep water fresh.

A skimmer is a mechanical filter that pulls debris from the pond surface, traps it for easy removal, and sends the water to biological filters at the head of the streams. At the head,

As the garden matures, it takes on a more naturalized appearance. The pond seems to have always been part of the landscape.

beneficial bacteria consume ammonia, nitrites, and other toxic elements from the water, making it crystal clear and robbing unwanted algae of their nutritional source.

The combination of mechanical and biological filters doesn't take the pond keeper completely out of the maintenance loop, but the two do reduce the amount of time required for pond maintenance. In addition to the filters, there is a drain— a bottom siphon actually—at the bottom of the deepest level of the pond. It's installed there because that's where the fish will spend the most time, so this area will collect the most waste. The bottom drain increases circulation at the bottom of the pond—an area that in large ponds may be difficult to keep in motion. The bottom siphon exits at the side of the pond, where it's easy to keep leaks from occurring.

PLANT LIST FOR THE LARGE WATER GARDEN

Code	Plant Name	Number
A	Ajuga 'Atropurpurea'	30
B	Arrowhead	1
	ASTILBE	
C	'Amethyst'	1
D	'Red Sentinel'	5
E	Bishop's hat (Epimedium 'Rose Queen')	3
F	Blue Fescue	14
G	Euonymus (Silver Princess)	2
	HOSTA	
H	'Krossa Regal'	4
I	'Francee'	3
J	Juniper ('Wiltonii')	5
K	'White Nancy' Lamium	1
L	Lotus	1
M	Lungwort (Pulmonaria 'Sissinghurst White')	3
N	Miniature cattail	7
O	Vinca	22
P	Water celery	16
Q	Water lily, any	5
R	Yellow flag	8
S	Blue flag	1
T	Rocks	

PLAN FOR A LARGE WATER GARDEN

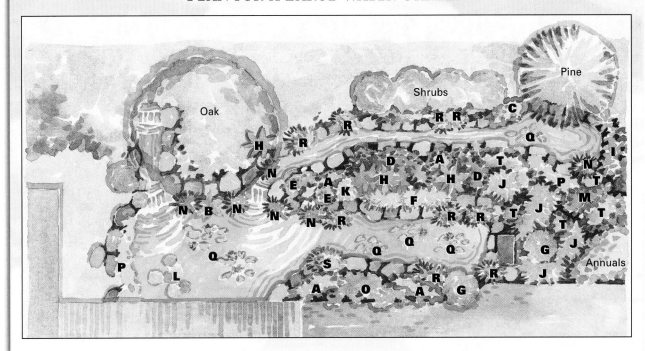

A POND WITH A BOG GARDEN

At the author's nursery, the bog garden keeps visitors from getting too close to the water's edge. In your yard, a bog can solve the problem of a low spot in the yard, ease the transition from pond edge to landscape, or simply provide a place to grow wet-soil lovers, such as lobelia.

Bog gardens are highly useful, but often overlooked, garden design elements. Incorporated at the edge of a pond, a bog is well-suited to informal or natural designs. A freestanding bog garden creates the perfect solution for a low or chronically wet spot where dryland plants won't thrive. When set with plants that prefer a wetter site than typically found in perennial gardens—plants such as lobelia and acorus—the bog provides an easy transition from pond edge to the rest of the landscape.

Most plants that do well as marginals also make fine bog plants. Water irises, cattails, and aquatic grasses are perfect choices at the water's edge. Further back from the water, perennials that tolerate moist soil, such as hostas and daylilies, grow well.

TRUE BOGS

Bog gardens have a double identity. To most gardeners, a bog garden is one that has moist soil, kept that way by an impermeable liner, and is planted with water-loving perennials. To a botanist, naturalist, or other specialist, a bog garden is a naturally occurring moist area with soil that is acidic and humusy and has little nutrient value. These true bogs are home to acid-loving, water-thriving species

such as cranberries; carnivorous plants including pitcher plants, sundew, and venus flytraps; and bog orchids, such as ladies' tresses and rose pogonia. Although well within the ability of home gardeners, true bogs create a different effect in the landscape, and the conditions and care they require are quite different, too.

BUILD A BOG

This is a typical gardener's bog. It was built to enhance the safety of a water garden. Because the owners were fearful that visitors or children might topple into the water, they recently rebuilt the pond to make it more stable and added a bog as a buffer between visitors and open water.

The pond is approximately 10 feet wide by 12 feet long and 2 feet deep. A 3-foot by 4-foot header pool, also 2 feet deep, is connected to the main pool by a three-step waterfall. Along one edge, the bog provides ample room for growing marginal water plants. Large, flat stones on the other edge provide a stable area for admirers to walk up to the water.

A skimmer box for filtration is opposite the waterfall at the northeast end of the pond. This allows prevailing winds, which are from the southwest, to blow floating debris into the skimmer box. To connect the tubing from the skimmer to the header pond, a shower drain was installed at the bottom of the header pool.

The main pond and the header pool are lined with rubber liner. Felt underlayment protects the liner in both areas as well as up into the bog edges.

The pond is edged with different sizes of locally available fieldstone placed in a natural arrangement around the pool. To give the impression that the pond is deeper than it is, a 6-inch-wide shelf that is 3 inches below the intended water line and filled with fieldstone rings the pond. This edging technique uses less stone. In addition, it makes the pond easier to clean.

Pieces of flat-sided stone were used for the waterfall. Because the stone had both flat and irregular faces, the owners dug out the shelf for the waterfall to accommodate the irregular sides, leaving the flat side facing upward. By doing this, they were able to have a flat waterfall made from rock that matched the edging. The owners also sprayed insulating foam underneath the rocks. This holds the rocks in place and forces the water up and over the rocks, rather than around or under them.

The bog planting pocket is roughly 2 to 3 feet wide and 6 to 10 inches deep and about

6 to 10 inches above the water line at the edge farthest from the pond. The underlayment and liner were placed in this pocket, then held in place at the far edge of the pocket with fieldstone. Then the pocket was filled in with clay soil. The pocket's pond-side edge is below the water line, so water filters into the pocket and keeps soil moist.

Water percolates through bags of lava rock in the bottom of the header pool. Beneficial bacteria colonize the lava rock, providing biological filtration for the pond. Floating plants, such as water hyacinth or water lettuce, serve as vegetative filters in the header pool. Because they are contained in the upper pond, they don't float helter-skelter in the main pond.

A pond of this size can hold up to five medium lilies and 25 to 50 bunches of oxygenators. Each spring three floaters are grown in the header pool and a mixture of hardy and tropical marginals are installed in the bog to ensure color all summer long.

FOR A TRUE BOG

Instead of filling a true bog with soil, use silica sand—the kind used in sandblasting or in pool filters. Limestone-based sand is harmful to the plants, because the lime forms compounds with other minerals in the sand, making nutrients unavailable to plants.

For a true bog you'll need to plant sphagnum moss. Sphagnum moss is the best indicator of the health of the bog. If it is turning brown and having trouble growing,

The acid soil in a true bog leads to a much different planting. Venus flytraps, sundews, and pitcher plants are typical of a true bog. Even the peat moss thrives.

Local fieldstone edges the pond. Set 3 inches below the water line, it gives the illusion of depth to the pond.

other bog plants won't grow either. If the moss is growing happily, other bog plants will also flourish.

First, place a few inches of premoistened, long-fiber, dried sphagnum moss on the surface of the soil. On top of that, place live sphagnum moss. You can use just the dry sphagnum moss, provided it has some green tips, which provide spores that will grow into live sphagnum moss. Additional sphagnum moss is likely to be attached to small carnivorous plants from the store.

Irrigate true bogs with acid (pH 6) water low in minerals. Distilled water or rainwater are good sources to start the bog.

PLANTS FOR THE BOG GARDEN

Code	Plant Name	Number
A	Water lily	2
B	Frog fruit	3
C	Arrowhead	3
D	Umbrella grass	3
E	Melon sword	2
F	Canna	1
G	Thalia	3
H	Bacopa	2
I	Water hyacinth	1
J	Water lettuce	1
K	Shrub	1
L	Ornamental grass	3
M	Annuals	

BOG GARDEN PLAN

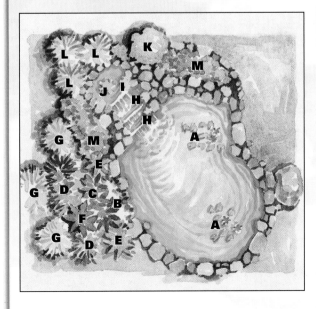

A CONTAINER WATER GARDEN

With a pond in a pot, you can have a water garden anywhere, even on a balcony.

Container water gardens are perhaps the easiest to start with. You can create one in an hour or two with no digging and little expense. And you can put them anywhere.

Virtually any kind of container works for a water garden. If it holds water—or can be made to hold water—it can become a water garden. Here are some suggestions: whiskey half barrels, galvanized buckets or livestock troughs (older ones that are no longer shiny, otherwise they can be toxic); oversize dishes and bowls, boulders or rocks with hollows, black plastic tubs designed for water gardens, wooden buckets, iron kettles, claw-foot bathtubs, even rubber boots.

IS IT WATERPROOF?

After choosing a container, check it for watertightness. Fill it with water and place it on a dry surface, such as a sidewalk or driveway. Let it sit for a full day, checking occasionally for leaks. If it does leak, seal minor cracks from the inside with aquarium-grade silicone sealant or caulk.

Make wooden and porous containers watertight with flexible liner or a brush-on sealant designed especially for water gardens. (You must seal or line whiskey barrel halves if they smell of whiskey to keep impurities in the wood from killing the fish.) If using flexible liner, fold and tuck it carefully into all recesses; staple or glue edges to the container with silicone sealer or rubber adhesive.

It is best to seal all containers with spray urethane, even pots that are glazed or galvanized. The urethane keeps terra-cotta pots from weeping, and it protects galvanized and iron containers from rust. Apply three coats to the inside of the pot, or enough to make it shiny.

PLANT THE CONTAINER

PLANTS: Choose plants for your container in keeping with its scale, such as fairy moss, miniature cattail, water iris, or 'Spiralis' rush. Plants that trail over edges, such as parrot's feather, with its feathery leaves and curling stems, also work well. Miniature water lilies such as 'Helvola', 'Rose Laydekeri', or 'Perry's Baby Red' are also good. Water-lily-like plants, such as water poppy or water snowflake, are good substitutes in container gardens. Frogbit makes a wonderful addition

1. Plug drainage holes with a scrap of liner spread with caulk. Fix cracks with caulk or sealant (aquarium-grade for pots with fish). Waterproof the inside of the pot with water-garden paint. It comes in black, white, or gray. Seal wooden containers with flexible liner.

2. Use a small fountain or aquarium bubbler to aerate the water. You'll need to match the pump to the pot's volume. To measure volume, fill the pot from 5-gallon buckets. Conceal the pump's cord and plug it into a GFCI (ground fault circuit interrupt) outlet.

as a floating plant. Miniature umbrella grass is in keeping with the container's small scale.

FISH: If you plan to stock your mini pond, you'll need to balance plant needs for sun with fish needs for oxygen. Most water garden plants do best with six hours or more of full sun per day. That much sun on a hot day heats up water significantly. In turn, the water becomes oxygen depleted, which stresses fish.

However, you can help fish get enough oxygen even in a warm site by positioning the container garden where it receives afternoon shade. Keep a thermometer in the water, and never let the water get warmer than 85° F. If fish surface to gasp for air, aerate the water immediately. Use a small, battery-powered aeration pump or an air stone, a device with a small external pump that's placed in the water.

Stock the pot with tropical fish or small goldfish. Mollies, platys, and swordtails are good choices for container water gardens. They handle high water temperatures and dine on mosquito larvae. Be sure to cover the container with netting to keep the fish from jumping out. Don't try koi in container gardens; they don't survive in such small areas.

Because the container garden will hold only a few fish, control the population by relocating offspring.

FOUNTAINS: Fountains help oxygenate water. The fountainhead and volume have to be just right, however. Avoid large, high sprays; choose a spray pattern in keeping with the container style. Small spitting fountains, such as a small fish or frogs that gently spray water into the pond, are well-suited for containers. Remember, too, that most floating plants don't like their leaves splashed, so you may have to choose between having fish and plants or a fountain.

You'll need only the smallest of pumps—a bubbler is a good choice. The pump should have an adjustable spray to fit the container. Drape its electric cord over the back, and hide it among plants or bury it under gravel.

3. Fill the container with water and let it sit for five to seven days to dissipate chlorine and stabilize water temperature. (Or use chlorine remover.) Where the water contains chloramines add chloramine remover. Stock with fish and plants after the water stabilizes.

4. Choose plants with a variety of shapes, textures, and colors. Include some that dangle over the edge and others, such as sedges, that are tall and spiky. You may need to set the smaller pots on bricks to raise them to the correct depth.

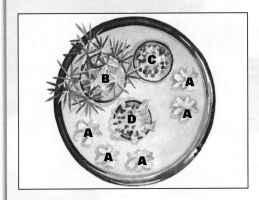

5. Add fish. Fish make an ordinary garden extraordinary. Let them adjust to the water by floating them in their water-filled plastic bag for 10 minutes before you release them.

AVOID COPPER

Copper containers are toxic to fish and other aquatic animals. They should not be used for water gardens unless they are lined with another material.

PLANT LIST FOR THE CONTAINER GARDEN

Code	Plant Name	Number
A	Water lettuce	5
B	Umbrella grass	1
C	Horsetail	1
D	Moneywort	1

PLAN FOR A CONTAINER

A PRIMER ON WATER GARDEN INSTALLATION

THE PARTS OF A GARDEN POND

Edging
This pond has a combination of pebble and rock edging.

Deep Zone to 36" deep
For overwintering fish and hardy plants in cold climates

Edging shelf
Underlayment
Liner

Marginal shelf
12" deep
For plants that prefer shallow water

Building a water garden is not a particularly difficult task, even for a beginner. All you need are a few basic tools. With two exceptions—electrical work and large excavations—you probably won't need to hire an outside contractor. For small jobs with straightforward electrical work, you may be able to wire the pond yourself, if such work is allowed in your community.

Excavation of even a small installation is often the most taxing part. The key to whether it's fun or frustrating lies in how much you can do by yourself without over-doing it. For an extra-large project, you're probably better served to contract out the work to someone with a backhoe. (Or rent one, if you have the skill to operate it.)

Water garden installation, like most home improvement projects, is easier to accomplish if you have someone to help. Whether you are installing liner, laying stone, hauling dirt, or just in need of a second opinion, a companion greatly speeds up the project.

As you launch into building your pond, allow plenty of time for each step. Most homeowners are overly optimistic with their estimate of the time it will take to complete a project. Anticipate unexpected complications, trips to the hardware store, and other time-consuming tasks. Take your time, and the installation can be almost as enjoyable as the finished product.

Building a pond is well within the skill level of most do-it-yourselfers. You can complete a small project in a weekend. One this size will take more time.

DIGGING

Excavation may be the most challenging aspect of creating a water garden. You can rise to the task, and even enjoy it, with some good planning. Allow plenty of time. Consider the pond size and soil type. An 18-inch-deep, 3×5-foot pond in sandy soil may take only an hour or two, but a 24-inch-deep, 6×10-foot pond in clay may take a weekend. Divide the digging into one-hour chunks with breaks so you don't strain your back.

Proper building techniques make the difference between a well-functioning water garden and one with chronic problems.

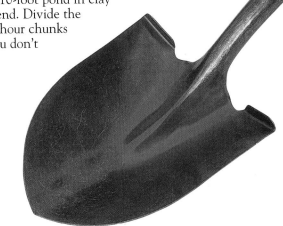

1. *Mark the outline of the pond with a garden hose or rope, or sprinkle a line of flour, fine soil, or garden lime. Live with the outline for a week or so to discover how well the new feature fits into the landscape and how it will affect traffic patterns.*

2. *Remove turf. Use it to fill bare spots in the lawn, set it aside in a pile of its own to compost, or use it as the base of a berm or a raised bed. Begin digging the hole for the pond, starting at the center and working toward the edge.*

3. *Toss soil into a wheelbarrow or onto a tarp to protect your lawn. If the soil is in good condition, use it to fill spots in the yard or build a slope for a waterfall, or haul it off. Don't leave it on the grass for more than a few days or it will kill the lawn.*

4. *As you dig, keep the pond edge level so the liner won't show. Check by resting a carpenter's level on a straight board laid across the pond. Work all around the pond, keeping one end of the board stationary to serve as a reference point.*

5. *Dig an optional shelf for the marginal plants about 12 inches deep. positioning it so the plants frame your view of the water garden. Then dig a ledge for the edging as deep as the edging material and slightly less wide.*

6. *In the coldest regions, you'll need an area in the pond that won't freeze in which to overwinter plants and fish. It should be 2 to 3 feet deep and as wide as it is deep. This deep area shouldn't be in the same spot you want to place a pump or fountain.*

INSTALLING FLEXIBLE LINER

Once flexible liner is in place and the pond partially filled, work the liner into the nooks and crannies of the pond.

One reason why flexible liner has become so popular for water garden installation is because it's easy to work with. However, you must install it properly to prevent it from showing (which speeds UV deterioration and makes your pond look unprofessional) and keep it from leaking.

After excavation, remove anything rough (roots, rocks, debris, glass) that might puncture the liner. Then spread underlayment—a layer of damp sand, old carpet, wet newspapers, or material made specifically for this use. This cushions the liner, adding to its life, and prevents punctures.

If you need to make a seam, do it before installation, using solvent cement or adhesive designed for this purpose. Lift the liner rather than dragging it, to avoid rips and punctures.

Don't leave the liner on the lawn in the sun. This can kill grass in less than half an hour. Wear thick socks and cotton gloves; the liner can get very hot in sunlight.

1. CUSHION THE HOLE WITH UNDERLAYMENT. *Use moist sand (horizontal surfaces only), old carpet, underlayment made for water gardens, or other materials. Cover both the bottom and the sides. At corners and curves, cut triangles in the underlayment to help fit contours.*

2. POSITION THE LINER. *Drape it loosely in the hole, arranging and pleating as needed. (This job may be accomplished faster and easier with two or more people.) Anchor the sides with bricks or stones, taking care to not stretch the liner.*

3. ADJUST THE LINER. *Add a few inches of water to the pond to settle the liner. Pleat and tuck the liner as necessary to make it fit the contours and corners of the pond.*

4. PREPARE FOR EDGING. *Fill the pond with a few more inches of water. Adjust the liner, then fill to just below the edging shelf. Trim the liner at the edge.*

5. INSTALL EDGING. *You can use flagstone, brick, cut stone, or other edging. Do a final trim of the liner. You can pat in a little soil behind the edging to conceal any visible liner.*

INSTALLING PREFORMED LINER

Preformed liner is a little more difficult to install than flexible liner. The key with preformed liner is to keep it supported under its entire surface. When you're working with flexible liner, you don't have to worry too much about the conformation of the hole—whatever it is, the flexible liner will conform to it. When you're excavating for a preformed liner, you have to get the hole to conform to the liner. Put the liner in and out of the hole several times during the excavation process to make sure that when it's finally in place, it is supported uniformly.

Preformed liners take much of the guesswork out of digging and lining a pond.

1. *Position the liner where you plan to locate the pond, using bricks if necessary to keep it level. Pound stakes in place around the liner and use them as guides to mark the exact outline. If the pond is small, make a template by tracing around the lip on cardboard.*

2. *Dig out the shape of the liner, making it 2 inches wider and 2 to 3 inches deeper than the actual liner. Conform your digging to the shape of shelves and deep areas, measuring depth, width, and level frequently. Monitor your work by lowering the liner into place and making adjustments.*

3. *Once the hole is dug, make sure there aren't any sharp objects or stones on the bottom. Fill the bottom of the hole with moist sand, fine soil, or a combination of the two. Use a short board to level the bottom. Tamp the soil down firmly and check the level once again.*

4. *Lower the liner into place, checking the level. You may need to remove the liner several times to make adjustments.*

5. *Fill the liner with 4 inches of water and begin backfilling. Firm the soil as you work. Add more water to the pond (no higher than the backfill). Backfill. Repeat. Install edging.*

Making a Bog

Bog gardens are among the easiest water gardens to install and maintain. A bog garden is simply a bed of moisture-retentive soil spread over a pond liner, which helps the soil retain water. In a bog garden, the soil is always wet.

Locate the bog next to your water garden so that it can tap into the supply of water in the pond. Ideally, the bog should be 3 to 4 feet in diameter and 18 inches deep. However, if necessary, it can be as shallow as 12 inches.

Use the same techniques to dig and shape the bog as described for installing a pond. The bog, however, doesn't need shelves along the edges; it is all one depth.

After lining the bog and building the dam, fill the bog with average garden soil.

Moisture-loving perennials such as variegated yellow flag, upper right, and primrose thrive in bog gardens attached to ponds.

1. *Dig a hole 6 to 18 inches deep in an area receiving at least 6 hours of sun a day. A low-lying or poorly drained area is perfect, as is a site next to a pond, where it's easy to keep the bog's soil moist.*

2. *Spread landscape fabric over the hole, or overlap large scraps of fabric. Pierce it every 3 feet or so with a garden fork. Spread 1 to 2 inches of pea gravel on the bottom of the hole. Trim the landscape fabric so it will be concealed under the soil surface.*

3. *To create a dam, build one of earth while you're digging, or make one of rocks between the bog and pond. Place landscape fabric between rock and soil to prevent soil from washing into the pond. Leave holes in the dam, or insert PVC pipe to create a passage for water.*

4. *Fill the bog with high-quality, moisture-retentive soil. You can also mix in sphagnum peat moss, but use it sparingly at first to see how plants react to it. Plant moisture-loving species in the bog and water them well. Fertilize occasionally with compost.*

CREATING A WATERFALL

A waterfall can be only a small splash down a few rocks into a tiny trough, or a trickle on the side of a pond. Or it can be an impressive cascade as part of an extensive stream. A waterfall can work alone or as one of several in a series.

A waterfall that is part of a stream has essentially three parts: the header pool, the lip over which the water falls, and the catch basin. Water collects in the header pool, then spills over the lip and into the catch basin (which can be a header pool for the next waterfall, if there is one).

When digging a waterfall, create a 12-inch shelf of compacted soil that extends into the streambed to support the weight of the waterfall lip and any stones on it. Or you can support the lip with boulders, concrete blocks, bricks, packed mortar, or poured concrete. Install underlayment and liner over the support.

If you build the waterfall with large rocks—a foot or more across—it will look more natural and be more stable if you prop the lip on a foundation stone, such as a rectangular piece of rock (or two) set vertically under the lip.

For a smaller water feature, you can build a mini waterfall. These designs can be very small, taking up less space than a bread box. You can build them to stand independently in the landscape or position them alongside a pond. However they're designed, they create a charming way to add splash and produce a cooling effect in your landscape.

To create a miniature waterfall on the side of a pond, install flexible tubing on the pump. Run the tubing to the intended site for the waterfall. Build up a small earth mound on which to position stones. Cover this mound with liner so the water flows back into the pond. Without the liner, the water can easily seep out between the rocks and never reach the pond. Stack the rocks on top of the liner.

You can create a lip and foundation stone for the waterfall, or you can arrange the stones in any manner. Turn on the pump periodically to see how the water flows over the stones. Use insulating foam as you would mortar to seal cracks and to direct the water flow.

You may want to purchase a preformed mini waterfall unit. Install it at the side of the pond with its lip slightly overlapping the edge of the pond, then pack loose soil and sand around it. Run the tubing the same way you would for a stone waterfall.

Once, you might have only dreamed you could have a water garden this beautiful. Now you can build it yourself. It takes planning and effort, but the end result will transform your backyard landscape.

Create a mini waterfall by laying stones or rocks in a pile. Position one stone, such as this large, flat one, to serve as the lip of the waterfall.

Set more rocks on the lip to hold it in place and form a natural-appearing outcropping. Run flexible tubing attached to a submersible pump in the pond up through the rocks. Adjust the flow to get the right effect.

WATER GARDENING RESOURCES

RETAIL & MAIL ORDER

Avian Aquatics, Inc.
P.O. Box 188
Harveson, DE 19951-0188
800-788-6478
www.avianaquatics.com
Water features for songbirds

Aqua Art Pond Specialists
11-G Poco Way, #154
American Canyon, CA 94503-1071
800-995-9164 (order line)
707-642-7663 (Helpline)
www.aquaart.com
Equipment, pond statuary, landscape
    accents, and filters

Crystal Palace Perennials, Ltd.
P.O. Box 154
St. John, IN 46373
219-374-9419
www.crystalpalaceperennial.com
Plants. Informative catalog: $3

Daydreamer Aquatic Gardens
225 Rumsey Road
Columbus, OH 43207
614-491-2978
www.daydreamergardens.com

Gilberg Perennial Farms
2906 Ossenfort Rd.
Glencoe, MO 63038
636-458-2033
Hardy and tropical water plants,
    supplies, and hardy perennials.

Green & Hagstrom, Inc.
P.O. Box 658
Fairview, TN 37062
615-799-0708
www.greenandhagstrom.com
Plants and fish, including koi

Lilypons Water Gardens
6800 Lilypons Road
P.O. Box 10
Buckeystown, MD 21717-0010
800-999-5459
www.lilypons.com
e-mail: info@lilypons.com
Plants, equipment, and supplies;
    informative catalog on items for
    sale as well as on the how-tos of
    water gardening

Lilypons Water Gardens
139 FM 1489
Brookshire, TX 77423-0188
800-999-5459

Maryland Aquatic Nurseries, Inc.
3427 North Furnace Road
Jarrettsville, MD 21084
410-557-7615
www.marylandaquatic.com
Plants, equipment, fountains for
    indoors and out.

Paradise Water Gardens
Route 18
Whitman, MA 02382
781-447-4711
800-955-0161
www.paradisewatergardens.com
Fish, plants, equipment and supplies

Pet Warehouse
P.O. Box 752138
Dayton, OH 45475
800-443-1160
www.petwhse.com; online catalog
Equipment and plants

Scherer Water Gardens
104 Waterside Road
Northport, NY 11768
631-261-7432
631-261-9325 (fax)
Fiberglass and polyethylene
    preformed pools and EPDM liners.
    Other equipment and plants.

Signature Ponds, Inc.
418 Liberty Lane
Jasper, GA 30143
706-692-5880
www.signatureponds.com
Lightweight alternative stones and
    boulders

Simple Gardens
615 Old Cemetery Road
Richmond, VT 05477
800-351-2438
www.simplegardens.com
Plants and containers for water
    gardens

Slocum Water Gardens
1101 Cypress Garden Blvd.
Winter Haven, FL 33884
863-293-7151
www.slocumwatergardens.com
Plants, equipment, goldfish and koi
Catalog: $3

Tilley's Nursery/The Water Works
111 E. Fairmount Street
Coopersburg, PA 18036
610-282-4784
www.tnwaterworks.com
Mostly retail; mail order through
    internet only

Van Ness Water Gardens
2460 North Euclid Ave.
Upland, CA 91784-1199
800-205-2425
www.vnwg.com
Equipment and plants. Catalog offers
    information on plant requirements
    and their uses and advice on water
    gardening. Catalog: $4

Varsity Pond Supplies
2112 Omega Drive
Santa Ana, CA 92705
800-700-1720
email: pspindola@earthlink.net
Tetra products for ponds and for koi

The Water Garden
5594 Dayton Blvd.
Chattanooga, TN 37415
423-870-2838
www.watergarden.com

Water Garden Gems, Inc.
3136 Bolton Rd.
Marion, TX 78124-6002
800-682-6098
210-659-1528 (fax)
www.watergardengems.com
Equipment and some plants. Well-
    organized and indexed catalog

Waterford Gardens
74 East Allendale Rd.
Saddle River, NJ 07458
201-327-0721
www.waterford-gardens.com
Plants, equipment, books, supplies,
    fish.
Catalog: $5

Wildlife Nurseries, Inc.
P.O. Box 2724
Oshkosh, WI 54903-2724
920-231-3780
Hardy-perennial aquatic and wetland
plants, available in quantities of
one to 1,000 stems

William Tricker, Inc.
7125 Tanglewood Dr.
Independence, OH 44131
800-524-3492
www.tricker.com
Water lilies, lotus and other water
plants, equipment, books, and fish.
Catalog: $2

SUPPLIERS AND DISTRIBUTORS (WHOLESALE)

Beckett Corporation
5931 Campus Circle Drive
Irving, TX 75063-2606
888-BECKETT
www.888beckett.com
National distributor of water garden
products. Website has an online
pond designer, which
automatically calculates pond
volume.

Little Giant Pump Company
P.O. Box 12010
Oklahoma City, OK 73157-2010
405-947-2511
www.littlegiant.com
Submersible pumps and related
equipment. Website lets you
design your water garden online
and directs you to local retailers.

Water Creations, Inc.
2507 East 21st St.
Des Moines, IA 50317
800-475-2044
email: info@watercreations.com
www.watercreations.com
Liners, pumps, filters, water
gardening products, fish and plants

Pond Supplies of America
1204A Deer Street
Yorkville, IL 60560
888-742-5772
www.pondsupplies.com
Skimmers, pumps, and other
equipment. Check website for

local retailers, installation
information, and downloadable
pond planner.

Tetra Pond
3001 Commerce Street
Blacksburg, VA 24060-6671
800-526-0650 X5433
www.tetra-fish.com
Aquatic planters, liners, pumps, and
fish supplies. Informational web
site for hobbyists.

Wicklein's Water Gardens
1820 Cromwell Bridge Road
Baltimore, MD 21234
410-823-1335
800-382-6716
www.wickleinaquatics.com
Wholesale to garden centers and
landscapers. Consumers can buy
online.

INTERNET ONLY

Aqua-Mart, Inc.
P.O. Box 547399
Orlando, FL 32854-7399
800-245-5814
Fax: 800-326-2643
www.aqua-mart.com

Fish2U.com
P.O. Box 851
Gibsonton, FL 33534
www.fish2u.com

Pond and Landscape Solutions, Inc
2899 E. Big Beaver, #238
Troy, MI 48083
Fax: 248-524-9059
email: sales@pondsolutions.com
www.pondsolutions.com
Online course explaining how to
create and care for ponds, water
gardens and fish.

PondMart
P.O. Box 1802
Beltsville, MD 20704-1802
301-931-9395
www.pondmart.com or
www.backyardponds.com

Ripple Farms Water Gardens
www.ripplefarms.com

MAGAZINES

Pondkeeper
1000 Whitetail Court
Duncansville, PA 16635
www.pondkeeper.com
Trade magazine for aquatic plant
nurseries, ornamental fish
hatcheries, landscape installers,
and retailers, with plenty of
information for the hobbyist.

Koi USA
P.O. Box 1
Midway City, CA 92655
www.koiusa.com

Water Gardening Magazine
P.O. Box 607
St. John, IN 46373
800-308-6157
www.watergardening.com
Website offers an extensive product
source list.

CLUBS, ASSOCIATIONS, AND SOCIETIES:

Aquatic Gardeners Association
71 Ring Road
Plympton MA 02367
206-789-5840
www.aquatic-gardeners.org
Members receive bi-monthly journal,
The Aquatic Gardener, devoted
primarily to aquarium plants.

International Waterlily & Water
Gardening Society
1401 Johnson Ferry Road, Suite
328-G12
Marietta, GA 30062
e-mail: iwls@aol.com
www.iwgs.org
770-517-5746 (fax)
Quarterly journal, annual meetings,
comprehensive website with active
chat rooms.

National Pond Society
3933 Loch Highland Pass NE
Roswell, GA 30075-2029
800-742-4701
www.@pondscapes.com
Bimonthly *Pondscapes Magazine*

INDEX

A number in boldface indicates a photograph or illustration only. An asterisk (*) denotes the encyclopedia entry.

METRIC CONVERSIONS

U.S. Units to Metric Equivalents			Metric Units to U.S. Equivalents		
To Convert From	Multiply By	To Get	To Convert From	Multiply By	To Get
Inches	25.4	Millimeters	Millimeters	0.0394	Inches
Inches	2.54	Centimeters	Centimeters	0.3937	Inches
Feet	30.48	Centimeters	Centimeters	0.0328	Feet
Feet	0.3048	Meters	Meters	3.2808	Feet
Yards	0.9144	Meters	Meters	1.0936	Yards
Square inches	6.4516	Square centimeters	Square centimeters	0.1550	Square inches
Square feet	0.0929	Square meters	Square meters	10.764	Square feet
Square yards	0.8361	Square meters	Square meters	1.1960	Square yards
Acres	0.4047	Hectares	Hectares	2.4711	Acres
Cubic inches	16.387	Cubic centimeters	Cubic centimeters	0.0610	Cubic inches
Cubic feet	0.0283	Cubic meters	Cubic meters	35.315	Cubic feet
Cubic feet	28.316	Liters	Liters	0.0353	Cubic feet
Cubic yards	0.7646	Cubic meters	Cubic meters	1.308	Cubic yards
Cubic yards	764.55	Liters	Liters	0.0013	Cubic yards

To convert from degrees Fahrenheit (F) to degrees Celsius (C), first subtract 32, then multiply by ⁵⁄₉.

To convert from degrees Celsius to degrees Fahrenheit, multiply by ⁹⁄₅, then add 32.

USDA PLANT HARDINESS ZONE MAP

This map of climate zones helps you select plants for your garden that will survive a typical winter in your region. The United States Department of Agriculture (USDA) developed the map, basing the zones on the lowest recorded temperatures across North America. Zone 1 is the coldest area and Zone 11 is the warmest.

Plants are classified by the coldest temperature and zone they can endure. For example, plants hardy to Zone 6 survive where winter temperatures drop to –10° F. Those hardy to Zone 8 die long before it's that cold. These plants may grow in colder regions but must be replaced each year. Plants rated for a range of hardiness zones can usually survive winter in the coldest region as well as tolerate the summer heat of the warmest one.

To find your hardiness zone, note the approximate location of your community on the map, then match the color band marking that area to the key.

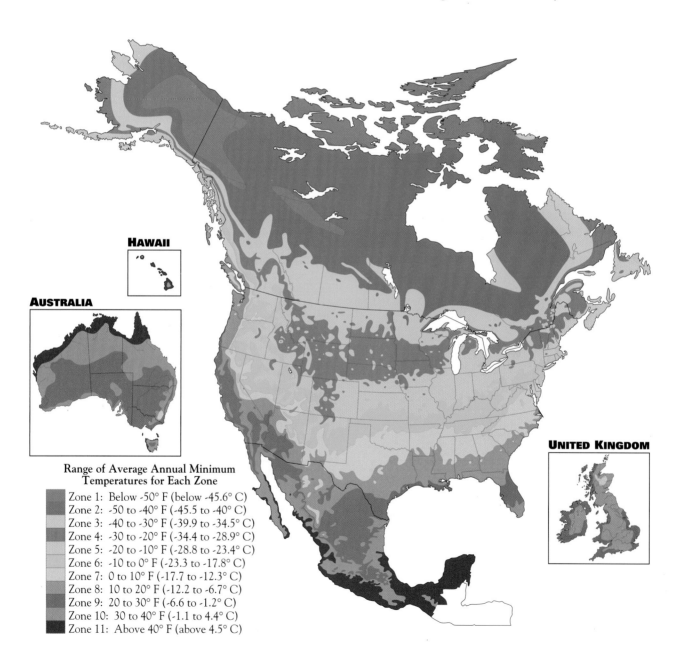

HAWAII

AUSTRALIA

UNITED KINGDOM

Range of Average Annual Minimum Temperatures for Each Zone

Zone 1: Below -50° F (below -45.6° C)
Zone 2: -50 to -40° F (-45.5 to -40° C)
Zone 3: -40 to -30° F (-39.9 to -34.5° C)
Zone 4: -30 to -20° F (-34.4 to -28.9° C)
Zone 5: -20 to -10° F (-28.8 to -23.4° C)
Zone 6: -10 to 0° F (-23.3 to -17.8° C)
Zone 7: 0 to 10° F (-17.7 to -12.3° C)
Zone 8: 10 to 20° F (-12.2 to -6.7° C)
Zone 9: 20 to 30° F (-6.6 to -1.2° C)
Zone 10: 30 to 40° F (-1.1 to 4.4° C)
Zone 11: Above 40° F (above 4.5° C)